LEARNING ABOUT THE OLD TESTAMENT

LEARNING ABOUT THE OLD TESTAMENT

A Biblical-Theological Introduction

Allan M. Harman

THE BANNER OF TRUTH TRUST

THE BANNER OF TRUTH TRUST
3 Murrayfield Road, Edinburgh, EH12 6EL, UK
P.O. Box 621, Carlisle, PA 17013, USA

❦

First published by Christian Focus Publications, Tain, Ross-shire, 2001
This revised edition © Allan M. Harman 2017

ISBN
Print: 978 1 84871 743 5
EPUB: 978 1 84871 744 2
Kindle: 978 1 84871 745 9

❦

Typeset in 10/14 pt Minion Pro at
The Banner of Truth Trust, Edinburgh

Printed in the USA by
Versa Press, Inc.,
East Peoria, IL

In memory of
Professor John Murray
mentor and friend

Contents

Foreword

THIS book originated in notes I prepared for students taking evening courses at the Presbyterian Theological College, Melbourne. It has gone through two previous editions, and has now been revised and slightly enlarged for this edition. My aim has been to show in outline how we can approach the Old Testament from the standpoint of biblical theology.

After each chapter I have listed some further reading. The decision has been made deliberately to select shorter, paperback books. Those out of print can be obtained from online booksellers such as bookfinder.com or bibliophile.com, or consulted in theological libraries.

As with all my other writings, I express my deep thanks to my wife Mairi for all her assistance, and to my friend, John M. Cromarty, for reading the manuscript and making comments. I also thank Téo Gamain for preparing the maps and diagrams.

Allan M. Harman
Wallington, Victoria
January 2017

Approaching the Old Testament

Our attitude to the Old Testament

When we take up a copy of the Old Testament, it is important to recognise that we must approach our reading and study of it in a different way from other ancient books. It claims to be God's word and demands our obedience. It is to be treasured and obeyed because of its origin and character. Only by the work of God's Holy Spirit are we convinced of this, because God's word comes to us as sinners.

Our attitude to it can be summed up in this way. We have to come to it

- *with reverence*—it is God's word as spoken and written by his servants, and it is to be handled and used with reverence.

- *with devotion*—it is a book that speaks of the wonderful truths about God and his works. Also, it contains many passages of praise that we can echo in our private and corporate worship.

• *with obedience* — it is a revelation of God's character, and of his demands upon us. The basic moral laws of the Old Testament carry over into the New Testament, and so still apply today.

The text of the Bible

Our main goal should be to get to know the text of the Old Testament. We cannot interpret the Old Testament without reading it! There is no substitute for a deep acquaintance with the thirty-nine books that make up the Old Testament.

Over the centuries God preserved the Scriptures in their original languages, and brought the manuscripts down to the present day. With meticulous care the Jewish scribes transmitted the Hebrew text to their successors. There is little variation between extant manuscripts of the Old Testament, a fact reinforced by the finding of the Dead Sea Scrolls. The initial finds, dating from 1945, were made public in 1947, and they came from manuscripts hidden in caves on the western side of the Dead Sea. They take the history of the Old Testament text back to 1,000 years before the time of Christ.

Bible translations

The need for translations of the Hebrew Old Testament became apparent before Christian times. The first Greek translation was made in Alexandria in Egypt, reputedly by seventy-two men brought down from Palestine. The legendary origin of this translation is reflected in the name by which it is still known, the Septuagint (Greek for seventy). It virtually became the Bible of the early Christian church, for Greek was the common language of the eastern Mediterranean world. Translations into other languages, such as Aramaic, Syriac, Arabic and especially Latin, followed. The Latin Bible, translated by Jerome and called the Vulgate, meaning the common version, was used by the church in medieval times, and it remains the official Bible of the Roman Catholic Church to the present day.

Once missionary work began, translations into many languages were needed. At the time of the Reformation, the major European languages became the vehicles for transmitting God's word. In English, the Authorised or King James Version was a major achievement, and it remained as the standard English version for over 350 years. Various revisions of it are now available including the Revised Standard Version, the New American Standard Bible, the New King James Version, the New Revised Standard Version, and the English Standard Version. The New International Version is a completely new translation into modern English. The Good News Bible is in more colloquial English, but lacks the accuracy necessary for study purposes. For our own use, we need to pick one of the good newer versions, and make it our Bible for regular reading and study. Constantly changing between versions militates against acquiring a thorough knowledge of the English text of the Bible.

The distinction between translation and interpretation must always be kept in mind. The Old Testament is an ancient document, and it requires careful translation. It is the role of teachers and preachers to convey its message in modern idiom to their contemporaries.

Perspective on the study of the Old Testament

Certain general principles need to be in our minds as we come to the study of the Old Testament. Without these principles we will become engrossed with difficult detail, make wrong application of laws, or fail to grasp the major themes.

It is essential to remember the *unity* of the Bible. Though composed of sixty-six books, the Bible forms a unity. It contains God's revelation given over a long period of time. However, the ultimate author of the Bible is God himself, and the theme that is central to it concerns himself and his relationship with the world he made. When any particular passage proves difficult to understand, we must turn to other passages where the truth is set out more plainly.

Guidelines

In studying the Old Testament revelation there are three main ideas about it that help to provide guidelines for us. These form the basis of a biblical-theological understanding of its contents.

1. God's revelation was *progressive*, for he did not reveal himself fully until the coming of Jesus. This is not to suggest that early revelation was false, and the later revelation true. Rather, the progression was from partial to complete, from preparatory to final. Another way to describe God's disclosures of his purposes is to say that revelation was cumulative. At each stage of the Old Testament, revelation was prospective, in that pointers were always given of further revelation of God's will and purposes.

4

2. God's revelation came *in stages*, and the Old Testament itself provides the markers that set off several major periods of revelation from each other. The major periods are signalled by the inauguration of fresh covenantal formulations. When we look at the history of the Old Testament we can see periods (such as the Exodus from Egypt) when God did so much for Israel, and also at that time revealed so much of his character and purpose.

3. God's revelation was *redemptive*, for the main purpose of divine revelation was to show how sinners can be redeemed and brought back into fellowship with God. Believers in the Old Testament enjoyed that experience of redemption as much as New Testament Christians. They were forgiven their sins because Jesus was ultimately to die as the perfect sacrifice both for those who lived before his death and those who lived subsequently.

The light of the New Testament is necessary to understand the Old Testament. It is the final revelation of God, and teaches us how to understand many aspects of earlier revelation. In it we find explanations given of practices and institutions, and, above all, we are taught how Jesus has fulfilled what was given in the sign language of sacrifice. God, who spoke in many different ways by his prophets, spoke finally in the coming of Jesus (Heb. 1:1, 2). Without the New Testament, our reading of the Old Testament would be like trying to understand a novel or play without having the final chapter to help us. The expectation of the Old Testament believers found its fulfilment in the person and ministry of Jesus.

Relationship of Biblical Theology to Other Disciplines

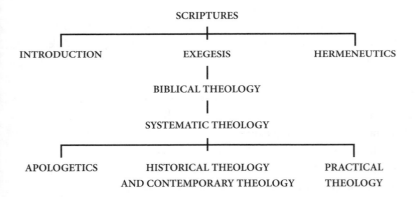

Importance of the Old Testament

Study of the Old Testament is important for Christians today. The foundational truths of the Bible are set out in the Old Testament, and in many cases they are pre-supposed by the New Testament writers. On the other hand, without a knowledge of the Old Testament, we cannot adequately explain much of the New Testament. While this is true particularly of books like the Epistle to the Hebrews, yet it also applies very widely to words and concepts that are rooted in the Old Testament (such as forgiveness, ransom, grace, redemption).

Two other comments need to be made. The first is that to understand the Old Testament we cannot be selective in our reading of its pages. The total flow of the history and thought of that period must be in our minds if we are to understand it. Knowledge of isolated stories does not give us the broad perspective that we need.

Secondly, as our understanding of the Old Testament increases, it should also increase our understanding of the New Testament. Moreover, our increasing biblical knowledge should stimulate us to go and tell the message of the Bible to others. Biblical study should result in the desire to bring others to share both our knowledge and our commitment to the Lord. Greater knowledge of our Redeemer should provide strong missionary motivation.

For further reading

- Sinclair B. Ferguson, *From the Mouth of God: Trusting, Reading, and Applying the Bible* (Edinburgh: Banner of Truth Trust, 2014).

- Wayne Grudem, C. John Collins, and Thomas R. Schreiner, editors, *Understanding Scripture: An Overview of the Bible's Origin, Reliability and Meaning* (Wheaton: Crossway, 2012).

- J. A. Motyer, *A Pocket Guide to Loving the Old Testament* (Fearn: Christian Focus, 2015).

2

Background to the Old Testament

The setting of the Old Testament

The Old Testament was written in the Near East, and so it has many features that reflect the varied cultural backgrounds from which it came. Study of these backgrounds helps us to understand customs that are referred to in the biblical text, and also words and phrases that mention things that are strange to us. The fact that God's revelation came in particular cultural settings need not surprise us, for the events of the Bible happened on actual calendar days and in precise geographical situations. The more we know about these situations, the better we are able to understand the significance of words and events. The development of modern archaeology has been of great assistance in shedding light on the ancient Near East.

Palestine was situated on the Mediterranean coast in a strategic part of the Near East. The name 'Palestine' has been taken over into English from the word 'Philistia', land of the Philistines. It was on convenient trade routes between Egypt in the south-west and countries such as Assyria in the north-east.

While we may think the climate harsh and the vegetation anything but lush, yet the Bible describes it as a 'land flowing with milk and honey'. In comparison with neighbouring countries, it was well-provided with water supplies and other natural advantages. From the Mediterranean coast, and also from the Gulf of Aqabah, there was sea access to other sources of supply of precious goods.

The geography of Palestine

The biblical text calls the land 'Canaan', after its inhabitants prior to the Israelite invasion, and the language of the Israelites (Hebrew) as 'the lip of Canaan' (Isa. 19:18). The land was promised to Abraham by God, and descriptions of its boundaries are given in various Old Testament passages (Gen. 15:18-21; Exod. 23:31; Josh. 1:4; Psa. 80:8-11). Basically these boundaries were Egypt in the south, Lebanon in the north, the Mediterranean in the west, and the Euphrates in the north-east. This territory was occupied in at least two periods of Old Testament history. During the reigns of David and Solomon the kingdom was extended to the promised borders, and then, during the reigns of Jeroboam II (c. 793–753 BC) in the north and Uzziah (c. 792–740 BC) in the south, the full territorial lands were under Israelite control.

The land of Canaan has five main geographical areas, four of them running north/south. The first is the rich coastal plain, broken only by the Carmel range jutting out to the sea. Secondly, there is the upland area stretching from the hills of Galilee in the north, down through Samaria, and finally embracing the Judean hills in the south. The only major break in this line of hills is where the valley of Jezreel extends from the Mediterranean just north of the Carmel range to the Jordan in the east. Thirdly, there is the Jordan valley, from Hermon in the north down to the Sea of Galilee, and from there the Jordan River continues to flow down to the Dead Sea. The Jordan today in this stretch has very little water in it, because its resources are tapped further north to provide water for much of Israel's irrigation system. The surface level of the Dead Sea is well below sea level (400m), with the floor at the deepest part being another 400m lower still. The sea has a very high salt content, which prevents any life existing in it, and from that it got its biblical name, 'The Salt Sea'. South of the Dead Sea the same rift valley continues down to the present-day port and tourist resort of Eilat. The fourth region is that of the hills of Transjordania, including Golan, Bashan, and Moab. The final geographical area is the Negev, the dry southerly region crossing the country from a line between Gaza and Beersheba. It extends from the hill country of Judah in the north to the Sinai Peninsula in the south, covering approximately half of the ground area of present-day Israel.

The geography of Palestine is important because it explains many references and incidents in the Old Testament. For example, the study of a map shows why sites such as those occupied by Jerusalem or Samaria were chosen. These were strategic ones with good natural defences. Geography dictated the trade routes, and this is why King Josiah was killed by the Egyptians at Megiddo in the valley of Jezreel (2 Kings 23:29, 30). He had clearly gone there hoping to prevent them from proceeding further.

The archaeology of Palestine

The limitations of archaeological discovery have to be recognised at the outset. In the Old Testament there is no continuous historical record that notes every major event. Many gaps exist in our knowledge. We must also remember that we are dealing with a Near Eastern text, not a Western one. This means that we cannot impose our criteria of historical writing on the Old Testament. Thus, it is a difficult task on many occasions to align the Old Testament record with the present state of knowledge derived from archaeology.

Another real limitation is that archaeology will never be able to provide convincing proof for the accuracy of the Old Testament. Two main reasons lie behind this statement. On the one hand, not every important site, or any site in its entirety, will ever be excavated. The task is just too extensive to allow that to happen. A tremendous amount of work has been done, but an even greater amount of evidence awaits investigation. On the other hand, archaeology can never provide proof of much of the Old Testament because it is composed of material not subject to proof. That is to say, much of the Old Testament is comprised of words that are claimed to be from God, or spoken by his servants the prophets. These words are not susceptible to proof by archaeological discovery.

For the Old Testament, the purpose of archaeology is not primarily to confirm the accuracy of the text. Some of the reasons for this have already been given. A more basic reason is that God's word cannot be proved by means of this kind. To say that we have to prove the Bible's accuracy before we believe it, is to place something in a position over the Bible. The Bible claims to be God's word, and we have to accept it on the basis of its own testimony, and as the Holy Spirit confirms this to our hearts. No human judge can validate its claims.

The main aim of archaeology

The main task of archaeology is to illuminate the Old Testament. This means that we look to archaeology to explain things that were difficult for us to understand before we had access to archaeological discoveries. It helps by clarifying the meaning of something that was previously obscure. Several good examples occur in the patriarchal narratives, such as the custom of a childless couple adopting a servant as an heir (Gen. 15:2, 3). According to documents from Ur and Nuzi, this was a common practice.

Archaeology also helps by illustrating what we already know. It makes more vivid, things we already understand, by providing examples that we can see or feel. What is observed in this way impresses the matters more firmly in our minds, and it gives us further parallels or background information. To visit a museum with a display of objects from the biblical world enables us to visualise to a greater degree what the every-day life of the people was like. A tour of Israel to see major sites and excavations brings a new dimension to our understanding of many parts of the Old Testament. However, such a visit should not be regarded as a necessary prerequisite for understanding the teaching of God's word, the inspired written Scriptures.

While the role of archaeology is not primarily to prove the Bible, yet archaeology does help by demonstrating the reliability and accuracy of the biblical writings. The biblical faith rests on the historical basis of the Bible. Advancing knowledge of archaeology provides complementary information from outside the Bible, and nothing has been found that can be proved to contradict any assertion in the biblical text. Archaeology itself is a developing discipline, and former investigations require verification and re-assessment. Archaeological research will continue to provide valuable help as we seek to understand what God has given us in the pages of the Old Testament.

For further reading

- O. Palmer Robertson, *Understanding the Land of the Bible: A Biblical-Theological Guide* (Phillipsburg: P&R Publishing, 1996).

3

God's Covenants

Covenants in the Old Testament

We are very used to the word 'covenant', because we often hear of
it in connection with the Lord's Supper: 'This cup that is poured
out for you is the new covenant in my blood' (Luke 22:20).
Another synonym is the word 'testament', that is common in
the New Testament, occurring over thirty times in our English
Bibles. Not only does the word 'covenant' occur frequently, but
the concept is of great significance for understanding the Bible.
It provides the markers that distinguish the various periods of
biblical history and revelation.

In the Old Testament 'covenant' is used of formal relationships between people, such as the one between David and
Jonathan (1 Sam. 18:3). However, the term is used most frequently to describe the relationship between God and men.
In quite a few cases there is a ceremony in which God and the
people, entering into the covenant relationship, give assent to
the demands of the covenant, or they pledge performance of
certain duties. Thus, we have a passage such as Genesis 15, that

describes a vision of God ratifying the covenant he had made with Abraham. Exodus 24 provides an illustration of a covenant where the people pledge their obedience to the Lord's demands. Right through the Old Testament, from the first book (Genesis) to the last one in our Bibles (Malachi), there is constant mention of God's covenant with his people. The word only occurs in the Old Testament as a singular noun, never as a plural, a fact that emphasises the unity of God's covenantal dealing with Israel.

Covenants outside the Bible

Like many other biblical words and ideas, 'covenant' was one that was well-known to people in the ancient Near East. Archaeology has helped here, in providing stone or clay tablets from various countries that detail how kings made covenants or treaties with conquered peoples. These treaties date from as early as 2,300 BC down to 700 BC. In particular, treaties made by the Hittites in the period just before the Israelites came out of their bondage in Egypt, show many similarities to those in the Old Testament. These treaties follow a set form that takes on this appearance:

a. An introduction explaining who the king is.

b. An historical survey explaining the background to the treaty.

c. Demands that the king made upon his subjects.

d. Provision for a copy to be placed in the temple of the people and for the regular reading of it.

e. Calling witnesses to bear testimony to the fact that the treaty had been made.

f. Curses or blessings that would follow, depending upon obedience or disobedience.

In addition to these features, which were provided in writing, there was also an oath. This was usually taken by following some set ritual. At times this took the form of a solemn meal (see Exod. 24:9-11; Josh. 9:14, 15).

Several Old Testament covenants show very strong resemblances to this pattern. This is so when we look at the covenant made with Abraham (Gen. 12; 15; 17), or the covenant at Sinai (Exod. 20–24), or the renewal of that covenant forty years later just before the children of Israel marched into the land of Canaan (the book of Deuteronomy). What happened was that God chose to give his teaching to Israel in a form with which they were already quite familiar. By using ideas from the secular realm and applying them in the spiritual realm, God was helping the people to grasp more easily the significance of their relationship with himself. He was the great king (Psa. 47:2) who had redeemed the nation from slavery in Egypt so that Israel would become his son and servant.

Covenant in the New Testament

The first appearances of the idea of the 'covenant' in the New Testament are in Luke 1, in the songs of Mary (the Magnificat, Luke 1:46-55) and of Zechariah (the Benedictus, Luke 1:67-79). Both sing of how Jesus' coming fulfils the covenant made so long before with Abraham. The word appears in the accounts of the Last Supper, in the Epistle to the Galatians, and most frequently in the Epistle to the Hebrews. The nature of a covenant clearly remains the same in both Old and New Testaments. The stress is on the wonderful grace of a sovereign God who comes to meet sinners in their need, and who enters into this special relationship with them.

The English Bibles at times use the word 'testament' (i.e. a will) to translate the word for 'covenant' that appears in the Greek New Testament. This is probably because of the way it is used in Hebrews 9:16, 17, where the idea of a will is definitely present. However, this is the only passage in the New Testament where we have to avoid the English word 'covenant'. Even here the same idea as a covenant is seen, in that there is no mention of an arrangement entered into after mutual discussion. Rather, the idea is that Jesus chose how his death would bring blessings to his faithful followers. As with the Old Testament, the New Testament speaks of how God stooped to help those who were helpless, and how he brought into being a new covenant through the blood of Jesus.

Definition of covenant

It helps us to understand the idea better if we attempt to give a definition of it. We have to look at the way the Bible uses the idea, and then state this clearly in a few words. It is an idea related to a relationship that God establishes. He normally gave promises in connection with a covenant, and the people had to pledge themselves to obey his commands. Thus, we can say that *a covenant is a bond between God and man, given by a sovereign God as an expression of his grace, and in this formal way he expresses the relationship that exists between them*. To be in a covenantal relationship with God is a great blessing, for God promises, 'I will be your God and you shall be my people' (Exod. 6:7; Jer. 7:23; Ezek. 11:20; Heb. 8:10).

Sometimes the Bible speaks about a covenant without using the precise word. This is because other words also suggested the idea, and terms like 'chose' or 'know' often come in contexts that are describing some aspect of God's covenant. In Amos 3:2, God charges his own people with their sin, and says, 'You only have I known of all the families of the earth.' This is clearly a reference back to God's choice of Israel and to the covenant that he made at Sinai. In 2 Samuel 7 God makes wonderful promises to King David, but nowhere in this passage is the word 'covenant' used. However, it is clear that it is a covenant, for when all the ideas are put into song in Psalm 89, the word 'covenant' appears several times (see verses 3, 28, 34, 39). Likewise the early chapters of Genesis have to be understood as a covenant. This is shown by the fact that the covenant with Noah only confirms the earlier covenant (Gen. 6:18). The New Testament supports that by the way in which it links Adam and Jesus together as covenant mediators (Rom. 5:12-14; 1 Cor. 15:21, 22, 45-49).

The people in the Old Testament were very familiar with the covenant idea. In the psalms and in the writings of the prophets the idea comes to the fore in many ways. From beginning to end the Old Testament reveals an understanding of God's steadfast covenantal mercies. All the literature of the Old Testament speaks of the covenant, and the idea is used to point forward to the coming of a new covenant when Jesus would come as Messiah (Jer. 31:31-34; compare Heb. 8:8-12).

For further reading

- O. Palmer Robertson, *Covenants: God's Way* (Philadelphia: Great Commission Publications, 1987).

- Jonty Rhodes, *Covenants Made Simple: Understanding God's Unfolding Promises to His People* (Phillipsburg: P&R Publications, 2014).

- John Zinkand, *Covenants: God's Claims* (Dordt College Press, 1984).

4

The Covenant of Creation

The declaration of God's lordship

The Bible opens in a very dramatic way. It presents us with a creator who made this world out of nothing. He only had to speak and things come into existence (compare Psa. 33:6; 148:5). Throughout the first chapter of Genesis, God's activity follows a pattern. He declared what he was going to do, then gave his command, the creative activity took place, and finally he pronounced it 'good'. In the context 'good' is not contrasted with 'bad.' Rather, it indicates that God looked over his creation and saw that what had come into being corresponded with his purpose. The whole narrative in Genesis stresses the sovereign creator who brought everything into existence by his great power.

All of creation was intended for a purpose. Thus, God designated the role of the sun and moon (Gen. 1:17, 18), and the dominion that man was to have over the rest of the created world (Gen. 1:28). All creation was directed to fulfilling his will, and every aspect of it pointed to its origin and Lord. The song of the twenty-four elders in Revelation is a beautiful expression of this idea: 'You are worthy, our Lord and God, to receive glory and honour and power, for you created all things, and by your will they were created and have their being' (Rev. 4:11).

The creation of man

The account of creation presents us with a series of days. Nowhere does the Bible fix the length of these days, and in Genesis 1 and 2 the word 'day' is used in at least five different senses in relation to creation (day versus night; first day/second day; the first three non-solar days; God's unending Sabbath day [Gen. 2:2, 3]; and 'day' to describe the whole creative period [Gen. 2:4]). A general parallel exists between the first three days, and the second three days. On the first three were created light, sea and air, and finally land and vegetation. Then, on the second three days we have the created things that rule over these realms —light bearers (sun, moon and stars), fish and fowl, and finally animals and man. The creation of mankind formed the climax of God's creative work. In Psalm 8, a song dealing with creation, it is not surprising that the psalmist, after looking at the world around him, exclaims, 'What is man that you are mindful of him, the son of man that you care for him? You made him a little lower than the heavenly beings and crowned him with glory and honour' (Psa. 8:4, 5).

While men and women are creatures of God like the animals, yet the difference between them is marked. They were made in God's image and likeness (Gen. 1:26, 27). As image bearers they have soul and mind, and they were created to have fellowship with God. The New Testament helps to explain what is meant by the image of God when it speaks of us being restored in Christ to God's image in righteousness and holiness (Eph. 4:24; Col. 3:10).

Mankind was appointed to rule in God's stead over the created world. The task was expressed as populating the earth and having dominion over it (Gen. 1:28). As the apex of creation, mankind was invested with authority over everything else that God had made. This general command in Genesis 1 is made more explicit when Adam is placed in the Garden of Eden 'to work it and take care of it' (Gen. 2:15). He had delegated authority from God over creation, but this meant caring for the creation as God himself would. The earth was mankind's to use wisely.

Mankind's original position in relation to God was one of fellowship and communion. This is shown by the fact that Adam and Eve were living in Eden, God's garden (Gen. 2:8; compare Ezek. 28:13). In the garden was the tree of life (Gen. 2:9), which will appear again in heaven when sin is no more (Rev. 2:7). Also, the garden was the place where God revealed himself to mankind by speaking with Adam and Eve, and appearing to them. There was nothing to mar the relationship between the first human couple and their creator.

Temptation and sin

In the sinless life of Eden a tempter appeared. The Bible does not explain the origin of evil. Rather, just as it confronts us with the creator in Genesis 1, so it confronts us with Satan in Genesis 3.

While God had a good design in view in allowing Adam and Eve to be tempted, Satan had an evil design. He wanted them to acknowledge him as lord of their lives, and in order to achieve that, he allured them away from commitment to God. The Bible often refers to the reality of this experience, and to the reality of the devil (compare the NT references in Matt. 13:38, 39; John 8:44; Rom. 16:20; 2 Cor. 11:14; 1 John 3:8; Rev. 12:9).

Satan worked cleverly in tempting Adam and Eve. He approached Eve first, and put in her mind the thought that God's prohibition of eating of the fruit was too comprehensive. When Eve began to doubt God's word, Satan flatly contradicted what God had said, and he tempted Eve to think she could be like God himself (Gen. 3:4, 5). When Eve was attracted to the fruit of the tree as desirable to her sight, appealing to the taste, and able to make her wise, she yielded to the tempter. Sin still has its attraction for sinners (James 1:13, 14; 1 John 2:15, 16). In turn, Eve became the agent in tempting Adam, and he too succumbed.

Sin brought with it immediate consequences. Being sinners, Adam and Eve were then no longer in fellowship with God. They realised they needed covering when in God's presence. They tried to make garments for themselves, and even to hide themselves when he appeared. What was needed was the covering that God would provide for them (Gen. 3:21). They now lost their happy relationship with God, and surrendered their right to be in God's garden (see Gen. 3:23, 24). The fact that they were sinners showed itself, with Adam even blaming Eve, whom he got from God, for his sin (Gen. 3:12).

Curse and blessing

Sin always brings judgment. So it was with the first sin. Immediately after interrogating Adam and Eve, God pronounced judgment. That judgment affected Satan, woman, and man. God's curse was expressed against Satan, who would be subjected to degradation. Those who followed him would have life-long antagonism towards those who trusted in God's word. Human life was to continue, but relationships would be distorted, and child-bearing and the production of necessary foodstuffs would now become arduous. The effect of sin was not to introduce a new principle (death), but to alter the existing relationships so that life became burdensome. No indication is given in the biblical text that animals, for example, were created immortal, while the instruction to Adam not to eat of the tree of life lest he die presupposes that he knew what death was (Gen. 2:17). The poetic description of creation in Psalm 104 speaks of the animals dying and returning to the dust (Psa. 104:29). Sin brought a radical change. Death, instead of working for man's good, was now to apply to man himself (Rom. 5:12). As soon as sin came, man was spiritually dead and subject also to physical death. Both Old and New Testaments teach that God is able to give new spiritual life, and that in Christ he has taken the sting out of death for Christian believers (1 Cor. 15:54-57).

But as well as judgment there was hope. Though Adam and Eve were banished from the garden, God's grace was extended to them, and this grace was expressed in various ways. When the account describes how God provided garments and clothed them, it is emphasising that it was God who moved to meet man in his need. When Eve bore Cain, she acknowledged that she had done so with the help of the Lord (Gen. 4:1). However, the greatest promise was that the offspring of the woman would crush the head of the serpent (Gen. 3:15). Martin Luther called this the first proclamation of the gospel. It held out the prospect that ultimately the seed of the woman, in the person of the Messiah, would crush Satan. That happened on the cross at Calvary, when Jesus disarmed the Satanic powers and authorities and made a public spectacle of them (Col. 2:15). The final vanquishing of Satan is yet to come (Rom. 16:20; Rev. 20:7-10).

For further reading

- Douglas Kelly, *Creation and Change: Genesis 1:1–2:4 in the Light of Changing Scientific Paradigms* (Fearn: Christian Focus, 2004).

- Rowland S. Ward, *Foundations in Genesis: Genesis 1-11 Today* (Wantirna: New Melbourne Press, 1998).

- E. J. Young, *In the Beginning* (Edinburgh: The Banner of Truth Trust, 1976).

- E. J. Young, *Genesis 3* (Edinburgh: The Banner of Truth Trust, 1984).

5

The Covenant with Noah

The progress of sin

The account in Genesis gives some positive indications of the faith and hope of mankind after the entrance of sin into the world. The first child born bears the name Cain, because, his mother said, he had been born with the help of the Lord (Gen. 4:1). Seth, the name given to the third son (Gen. 4:25), contrasts the sin of Cain in killing Abel with what God put in his place (Seth means 'put'). Worship of God is expressly mentioned in the reference to men calling on the name of the Lord (Gen. 4:26). But the consciousness of the effects of sin seem to have been present, for when Noah is born, Lamech his father said: 'Out of the ground that the LORD has cursed this one shall bring us relief from our work and from the toil of our hands' (Gen. 5:29). The earlier part of chapter 5 was concerned with the genealogy of Adam. Just as God had created him in his image (Gen. 1:26), so Adam procreates in his own image (Gen. 5:3). However, the genealogy states one of the effects of sin, in that it records that each person mentioned *died*. The only exception to this was the godly Enoch, whom God took away without his passing through death.

The general picture given of human life is one of degeneration and rebellion against God. Thus, Cain kills his brother, and is condemned to wander about like a vagrant (Gen. 4:1-16). By the time the seventh generation is reached with Lamech, God's provisions for man, as set out in chapters 1 and 2, are abused. Lamech takes two wives, and proudly boasts of his killing a young man who wounded him (Gen. 4:19, 23, 24). His character is in marked contrast to his opposite number in the line of Seth, Enoch, who walked with God (Gen. 5:22, 24). The expression, 'walking with God', denotes a life of close spiritual communion with God.

The degeneration reached its climax in the situation described in Genesis 6:1-7. The best interpretation of the early verses in this section is that rulers (called 'sons of God') were engaging in polygamy (marrying whom they would). Because they long for a name (i.e. a reputation, verse 4), they abuse their office, and allow their sinful desires to go contrary to God's ordinances. Like their forefather Lamech, they will not be constrained by God's basic pattern for human life.

Noah, the covenant servant

The character of Noah is important, for he was a righteous man, being set apart from his own generation by his blameless life (Gen. 6:9). He had a very close relationship with God that is described, as in Enoch's case, by the words 'walking with God'. As far as God's commands were concerned he was obedient, and he carried out explicitly the instructions he was given (see Gen. 6:22; 7:5, 16).

God in his grace came to Noah and warned him of his impending judgment upon the world because of mankind's sin. Wickedness had multiplied, and men were perpetually turning to evil (Gen. 6:5, 11). Noah was instructed to make an ark to save his family and the various animals that God specified. The New Testament points out that Noah acted out of faith, because he could not see the things about which he was warned. However, his obedient action was in itself an act condemning the world for its sin and unbelief (Heb. 11:7).

God called the relationship between himself and Noah a covenant, saying that he was confirming *his* covenant (Gen. 6:18). This implies that the relationship established at creation with humanity was indeed a covenant. Hence, we have commands given in Genesis 1 re-issued to Noah at the time of the flood (Gen. 9:1, 7). Despite the sinful condition of mankind, God intended to maintain the covenant relationship. The stress on God's initiative in the matter becomes even clearer from Genesis 9, where God emphasises in verses 9-17 that the origin of the relationship was with himself.

The account of the flood is given in Genesis 7:1–8:19. The description of the flood permits one to interpret it either as universal in extent, or else one that was geographically more limited, covering a limited but vast area occupied by humanity described in the previous chapters in Genesis. At present the evidence seems to favour the latter, with geological investigation supporting massive local floods but not a universal one. The Bible stresses that the flood was God's instrument of judgment, and that every living creature, except those in the ark, perished (Gen. 7:21-23; 2 Pet. 3:6, 7). The account speaks of what would have been seen and experienced by ordinary observers if they had been there in Noah's time.

The new order

God in his grace preserved all who were in the ark. He 'remembered' them (Gen. 8:1) and he brought them out of the ark. God's concern was for mankind, but also for all the animals in the ark. They too were the objects of his mercy and included within the covenant he was making (verse 21; Gen. 9:9, 10; see also Psa. 104:27, 28; Psa. 145:9, 15, 16; Jon. 4:11). His grace was to continue till the end of time (note the double occurrence of 'never again' in Gen. 8:21), while the Lord indicated that the earth was not going to endure for ever (verse 22).

The reason why God would not again destroy the world is stated in this way in verse 21: 'I will never again curse the ground because of man, for the intention of man's heart is evil from his youth.' This may seem surprising because it is practically the same as the reason recorded in Genesis 6:5 that God gave as he announced the coming of the judgment of the flood. Mankind's sinful heart was not changed by the flood, but remained the same. It was going to take something quite different to alter it. Later in the Bible we learn of the way in which God would give a new heart (Ezek. 36:26), and recreate to make all things new (2 Cor. 5:17).

After the flood, God gave very clear directions regarding several aspects of human life.

- Human life was to continue, and would never again be destroyed in the way it had been. In particular, the command given to man in Genesis 1:28 to populate the earth is now repeated twice (Gen. 9:1, 7). Sin would continue to manifest itself in the form of violence against other human beings.

- Human life was precious, because man was made in God's image. All life was God's, but especially human life. Therefore, to attack a fellow man was the same as attacking God. Provision was made for society to control acts against other humans, with the basic principle being that the punishment must not exceed the crime (Gen. 9:5, 6).

- Human life was to be sustained. This is implied in the command to fill the earth, but specific provision was made for man's physical needs (Gen. 9:2, 3). Sin brought disturbance into the natural world, but still the basic situation of Genesis 1 was to continue, in that man was to have dominion, and was able to use everything in God's world.

In confirming his covenant, God also gave a sign. The rainbow, chosen now as the sign of God's covenant (Gen. 9:12-17), was probably already in existence, but it was given new meaning as it was consecrated to serve in this particular way. Its main reference is not to us but to God, for he sees it and remembers his covenant. God cannot forget, but this sign emphasised how absolute God's promises were. Because it is a sign visible to us, it also reminds us of God's promise not to bring again a judgment by water as happened in the flood. The Hebrew word used in this passage for 'rainbow' is the usual word for a battle-bow, and so there may be present the idea that after the storm of the flood God is setting aside his judgment and showing his mercy and grace. When the Lord spoke through Isaiah of his promise that the waters would not again cover the earth, he promised that 'my steadfast love shall not depart from you, and my covenant of peace shall not be removed' (Isa. 54:9, 10).

For further reading

- F. D. Kidner, *Genesis: An Introduction and Commentary* (Tyndale Series: London: Tyndale Press, 1971), pp. 83-104.

- Rowland S. Ward, *Foundations in Genesis: Genesis 1-11 Today* (Wantirna: New Melbourne Press, 1998), pp. 141-186.

- Ronald F. Youngblood, *The Book of Genesis: An Introductory Commentary* (Grand Rapids: Baker Book House, 1991), pp. 79-123.

6

The Covenant with Abraham

The call of Abraham

The God of glory, as he is called by Stephen in Acts 7:2, appeared to Abram (meaning 'exalted father', but renamed Abraham, 'father of many', Gen. 17:5) in his home in Ur. He was instructed to go out and proceed to the land that God would show him (Gen. 12:1). That meant first of all going to Haran situated north-west from Ur. There he stayed until the death of his father Terah, when he set out with his wife and his nephew Lot for the land of Canaan to the south-west of Haran. The earliest translation of the Old Testament (the Greek Septuagint of about 250 BC) rightly calls him 'Abraham the migrant'. Although he did not know where he was going when first called, Abraham obeyed, and 'by faith he made his home in the promised land like a stranger in a foreign country' (Heb. 11:9). As with the earlier covenants, it was God who took the initiative, and who made known his commands and promises to Abraham.

Behind the call of Abraham lay the desire of God to have a people who would be separated from others as his own special people. God called him to leave the culture and community he knew so well. He was to become a recipient of God's revelation, and in order to be a channel of knowledge of the true God, he had to forsake the environment in which he had been raised. From the outset, Abraham had to learn that there was a distinctiveness about commitment to the living God. Severing himself from home and family, he had to make Jehovah (or Yahweh, the LORD) alone his support and stay.

God's covenant with Abraham

The covenant God made with Abraham is probably the one covenant referred to more often than any other in the Bible. There are three chapters in Genesis (12; 15; 17) that deal with this covenant. Perhaps chapter 12 anticipates the very important covenant ceremony detailed in chapter 15, while chapter 17 amounts to a confirmation of what has already been promised. Chapter 15 records a ceremony, in which God, in visible form, passes between dismembered pieces of animals. This type of ceremony was well-known as a way of taking an oath in the ancient Near East. In this case God was pledging himself to fulfil all that he had promised to do for Abraham.

Abraham was given something far more than just an inward sense of God's call. His religious life rested on great objective facts, for God promised certain things to his faithful servant. The stress was not on what Abraham would do for God, but what God would do for Abraham. All these promises involved great faith on Abraham's part, and he was tested in regard to each one. They were:

- that the chosen family was going to become a great nation (Gen. 12:2; 15:4, 5; 17:5, 6). He and Sarai (later called Sarah, Gen. 17:15) at that time were childless, but they were strengthened in faith and were persuaded that God had the power to do what he had promised (Rom. 4:20, 21; Heb. 11:11, 12). Abraham declared his Amen to what God promised, and it was counted to him for righteousness (Gen. 15:6; compare Rom. 4:3, 9). This was the first of the promises fulfilled. God gave them Isaac, and then many descendants.

- that the land of Canaan was to be his family's possession (Gen. 12:7; 15:7; 17:8). This territory extended from the river of Egypt to Lebanon, from the Mediterranean to the Euphrates (compare Josh. 1:4), and it was occupied during the reigns of David and Solomon. From Genesis 12 onwards the theme of the land is a major concern, until the conquest is recorded in the book of Joshua.

- that in Abraham all the families of the earth would be blessed (Gen. 12:2, 3; 22:18; 26:4). Some of the references to this blessing suggest that people would ask God to bless them just as he had blessed Abraham (Gen. 18:18; 28:14). Most references to it, however, imply that through Abraham's descendants God would bring blessing to the nations. The New Testament tells us this is what happened when Jesus came (Gal. 3:14).

These covenantal promises to Abraham were repeated to Isaac (Gen. 26:2-5, 24) and Jacob (Gen. 28:13-15; 35:9-12). The three names are often linked together when reference is made to these great promises (e.g. in Exod. 2:24; 3:6, 15-17; Deut. 9:27; 2 Kings 13:23; Psa. 105:6-11).

The rite of circumcision

As a sign of this covenant God commanded the rite of circumcision to be performed on all the males in Abraham's family, and thereafter on all male children. If obedience was not shown to this requirement, then death would follow. The language used plays on the fact that the expression in Hebrew for 'make a covenant' is really 'cut a covenant'. The penalty was to be cut off from Israel, so that it would no longer be just a token sign, but the real thing. The sign was a token one carried in the flesh of every male Israelite. It was a constant reminder of the need to keep God's covenant, and thus enjoy his blessing, or else suffer the consequences of disobedience. Later in the Bible the idea of circumcision was used in a wider sense. The heart had to be circumcised before God, for ultimately a true Jew is not one outwardly but one inwardly, 'and circumcision is circumcision of the heart, by the Spirit' (Rom. 2:29).

God's revelation to Abraham

As compared with the earlier periods, during the time of Abraham, God revealed himself frequently by speech (God 'said', or 'called to him'). He also gave revelation of himself by means of visible appearances. The common name for God was El Shaddai, that means the all-powerful one. From the Latin translation 'omnipotent' we get our English word 'almighty'. It is interesting that El Shaddai is used so often in the part of Genesis dealing with Abraham's life, for so many things in his experience went contrary to nature. In no way could Abraham bring God's promises to realisation. They needed the almighty power of God himself for their fulfilment. When Abraham suggested that perhaps Ishmael could be considered the child of promise, he had to learn that a supernatural act was needed to achieve God's purpose (Gen. 17:17-19). Abraham, conscious of his own inability to fulfil what was spoken of in the promises, must have been greatly encouraged by all the teaching he was given of the character of El Shaddai.

During Abraham's life there were several appearances of the angel of the Lord. These include the angel appearing to Hagar (Gen. 16:7-13), the three men who appeared to Abraham at Mamre (Gen. 18:1-33), and the angel who spoke to Abraham on Mount Moriah (Gen. 22:11-19). Later the angel was to appear to Jacob, Moses, Balaam, and others. The angel said he was God's messenger, but yet made claims that only God could make. The appearances were a true revelation of God and specifically one in human form. The fullest expression of the idea behind these appearances came when Jesus was born. He was truly human as the son of Mary, yet truly God manifest in the flesh.

Abraham's faith

Abraham's response to God's revelation was one of deep faith and intense spiritual vision. The Epistle to the Hebrews highlights Abraham's faith and his response to the events in his life. He was a true pilgrim, who realised that his accommodation in Canaan was merely temporary, and therefore lived there like a stranger in a foreign land. He had been promised the land, but yet he had to live in tents, and he had even to buy a burying place for his wife (Gen. 23). His real hope was set on something else, for he was looking for the city of the living God, that 'city that has foundations, whose designer and builder is God' (Heb. 11:9, 10).

For further reading

- Iain M. Duguid, *Living in the Gap between Promise and Reality: The Gospel according to Abraham* (Phillipsburg: P&R Publications, 1999).

- William J. Dumbrell, 'The Covenant with Abraham', *Covenant and Creation: An Old Testament Covenant Theology* (Milton Keynes: Paternoster, 2013), pp. 59-105.

- Ronald F. Youngblood, *The Book of Genesis: An Introductory Commentary* (Grand Rapids: Baker Book House, 1991), pp. 135-203.

7

The Exodus

Israel in Egypt

The book of Genesis recounts the basic information about the lives of the patriarchs, Abraham, Isaac and Jacob. In making his covenant with Abraham, God had said that for 400 years Abraham's descendants would be enslaved in a foreign land until God punished their captors. Israel would then come out with many possessions (Gen. 15:13, 14). The latter part of Genesis tells how Jacob's favoured son, Joseph, was sold to Egypt, and how he was put in charge of the land (Gen. 41). Ultimately Jacob and his family joined Joseph and his wife and two sons in Egypt, making seventy persons in all (Gen. 46:26, 27; Exod. 1:5. The figure of seventy-five in Acts 7:14 is taken from the Septuagint. It omitted Jacob and Joseph from the list, but included nine sons of Joseph.)

The time spent by the Israelites in Egypt was 430 years (Exod. 12:40, 41), and for the majority of that period there is no biblical commentary covering it. The fewness in numbers of Israel when they first arrived in Egypt contrasts markedly with the large increase in size just before the exodus (Exod. 1:6-22). God had fulfilled his first promise to Abraham, and he had made his descendants into a great nation. The size of Israel presented a problem to the Egyptians, especially if the Israelites ever sided with an invading army (Exod. 1:10). Hence they began to oppress them, and made them supply labour, including that needed for the building of the store cities of Pithom and Rameses. This oppression failed to reduce the numbers, and so the Hebrew midwives were instructed to kill all the Hebrew boys at birth. The manner in which the decree was evaded sets the background for the story of the birth and upbringing of Moses.

In their distress Israel had not been forsaken by God. They cried to him, and just as God had 'remembered' Noah because of his covenant (Gen. 8:1), so he 'remembered his covenant with Abraham, Isaac and Jacob' (Exod. 2:24; see also 3:16, 17; 6:5). He was going to fulfil his promise of bringing them out of their slavery, and he would do so in a way that would reveal his grace and power.

The call of Moses

Moses' parents trusted in the Lord, and they took steps to save their son. After being rescued from his basket in the reeds along the Nile, by God's providence he was looked after by his own mother until he became virtually an adopted son of Pharaoh's daughter (Exod. 2:1-11). While in Pharaoh's house he was educated in all the learning of the Egyptians, and he became powerful in speech and action (Acts 7:22). At the age of forty, he saw one of the Hebrew slaves being beaten. He intervened and killed the Egyptian, but when he found out that other Hebrews knew about his action, he fled to Midian. He thought that by his own power he could release his people from slavery. Instead, he had to learn that deliverance would only come by the power of God (Acts 7:23-29).

Forty years later, while tending his father-in-law's flock, God appeared to him by means of the angel of the Lord (Exod. 3:1-6). He saw a bush burning, but it was not burnt up. When he approached it, God spoke to him from it, and several important truths were taught to him. Before he could act as God's servant to rescue his people he had to know:

- that God was holy. The angel of the Lord spoke to him as God himself, instructing him to take off his sandals, because in standing in God's presence he was on holy ground. He also hid his face, because he was frightened to look at this manifestation of God (verses 3, 5, 6).

- that his God was the covenantal God of his forefathers, Abraham, Isaac and Jacob. In making this declaration, God referred back to the promise to Abraham concerning his people coming up out of the land of slavery (verses 6, 8, 17).

- that this covenantal God was to be known by a special name. It was so special that the Jews did not pronounce it. In our English Bibles it is printed as LORD, and it appears also in an Anglicised form as Jehovah. The name meant that he was the loving and gracious God who was going to show his nature in redeeming his covenantal people.

- that he was to be God's messenger, and the one through whom God would deliver his people. He had to speak God's word to both the Israelites and to Pharaoh. Moses was not an eloquent speaker, and, therefore, his brother Aaron acted as his spokesman (Exod. 4:10-17).

- that God would display his power against the Egyptians. God used a variety of words to describe his actions —'redeem', 'deliver', 'bring out'. All these terms emphasised that it was only God who could release the people from their bondage.

God's deliverance

God's power was shown in so many ways to Israel and to the Egyptians. He performed miraculous signs for Moses (Exod. 4:1-9), and before Pharaoh (Exod. 7:6-13). He had assured Moses that he would strike the Egyptians with all his wonders (Exod. 3:20). This happened when he sent the series of plagues on Egypt, and they demonstrated his power over all of Egyptian life. This is why God called them 'my miraculous signs and wonders' (Exod. 7:3). They were also direct attacks on the religious life of Egypt, because the Egyptian gods were so bound up with the course of nature. The plagues were a judgment on the gods of Egypt (Exod. 12:12).

On the night of the last plague (the destruction of the first-born), the Israelites were finally commanded by Pharaoh to leave his country. God went ahead of them in the form of the pillar of cloud by day and the pillar of fire by night. When they were pursued by the Egyptians, both the angel of God and the pillar of cloud came round behind them and protected them (Exod. 14:19, 20). The Egyptians were destroyed by the waters of the Red Sea, but the Israelites were saved by the Lord. This does not appear to have been the present Red Sea, but a considerable body of water further north, probably more in the area of the Bitter Lakes. The Hebrew text of the Old Testament refers to it as the Sea of Reeds. After their deliverance they sang the Song of Moses that commences: 'I will sing to the LORD, for he is highly exalted. The horse and its rider he has hurled into the sea. The LORD is my strength and my song; he has become my salvation' (Exod. 15:1-17).

The exodus was also a wonderful demonstration of God's grace. The difference between Egypt and Israel was not that one was better than the other. Instead, it was because God, having set his love on the Israelites, had chosen them to be his people, and he had redeemed them from their slavery (Deut. 7:6-9). The institution of the Passover, with the sprinkling of the slain lamb's blood on the door frames, was to be an annual reminder of God's mercy in passing over or sparing the Israelites when he brought the final plague on the land. The great lesson being taught by this ceremony was that only through the shedding of blood was there forgiveness of sins and acceptance with God. The Passover had much in common with the peace offerings, for it involved a communal meal as a symbol of the fellowship that the participants enjoyed with God. The Passover anticipated the far greater sacrifice of the Lamb of God who takes away the sin of the world (John 1:29). Jesus came as the final passover lamb when he offered up himself as a sacrifice for his people (1 Cor. 5:7).

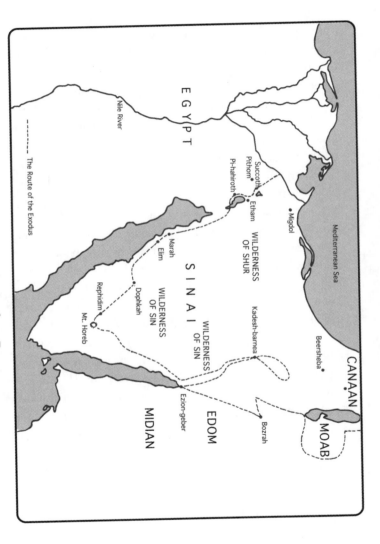

The Route of the Exodus from Egypt

For further reading

Iain D. Campbell, *Opening Up Exodus* (Leominster: Day One Publications, 2006).

Bernard Ramm, *His Way Out: A Fresh Look at Exodus* (Glendale: Regal Books, 1980).

John White, *Slavery to Servanthood: Tracing the Exodus throughout the Scripture* (Philadelphia: Great Commission Publications, 1987).

Ronald Youngblood, *Exodus* (Eugene: Wipf & Stock, 2000).

8

The Covenant at Sinai

The position of Israel before God

The making of the covenant on Mount Sinai came at a decisive point in Israel's history. Behind lay the exodus from Egypt and the experiences that the pilgrim people had been through as they moved down the peninsula to Sinai itself. This covenant marked a new stage in Israel's history, because it was a covenant with the nation, and not with individuals such as Noah or Abraham. It did not abolish what had been established by the earlier covenants but rather supplemented them (see Paul's words in Gal. 3:15-22). The later historical songs incorporated in the Psalter make this plain (Psa. 105:8-12, 42-45; 106:45).

Just as the covenant was about to be made, God reminded Israel of all that had happened during the exodus. He declared: 'You yourselves have seen what I did to the Egyptians, and how I bore you on eagles' wings and brought you to myself' (Exod. 19:4). He then called for their full obedience and observance of his covenant. After the regulations of the covenant were set out (Exod. 20–23), the people responded to the Lord and said: 'All

that the LORD has spoken we will do, and we will be obedient'
(Exod. 24:7). God would keep his covenant even when his people were unfaithful, but to enjoy the blessings of the covenant
the obedience of the people was essential.

Out of all the nations God had chosen Israel, and this choice
was to sonship. The relationship between God and Israel was
unique. Pharaoh had been told: 'This is what the LORD says:
Israel is my first-born son, and I told you, "Let my son go that he
may serve me"' (Exod. 4:22, 23). Some of the important features
of Israel's relationship with God are set out in Exodus 19:3-6.
As a first-born son, Israel was in a position of special privilege
and responsibility. God said that Israel was his 'treasured possession', and this same expression is repeated three times in
Deuteronomy (7:6; 14:2; 26:18). In addition, Israel was to be 'a
kingdom of priests' to God and 'a holy nation'. The first of these
expressions suggests a worshipping and serving community,
while the second reminds us that Israel as God's son had to
reflect his character. The people were to be holy, just as he was
holy (Lev. 19:2). The language of Exodus 19 is taken over into the
New Testament to describe the Christian church. Peter wrote
to the Christians scattered throughout Asia: 'You are a chosen
people, a royal priesthood, a holy nation, a people belonging to
God, that you may declare the praises of him who called you out
of darkness into his wonderful light' (1 Pet. 2:9).

The covenant confirmed

On Mount Sinai God confirmed the covenants he had already
made, and now added additional commitments for the people to

observe. Once again the emphasis is on God's initiative in dealing with his people. He called them to meet with him at Sinai, where he identified himself as the God who had redeemed them from the slavery of Egypt (Exod. 20:1, 2). The circumstances of God's revelation of himself stressed both his majesty and power, and the descriptions of entering into a covenant with him stress its solemnity (see the descriptions in Exod. 19:16-25; Exod. 20:18, 19; Deut. 5:22-27). God chose to use a form of covenant well-known to the people of that day, having strong similarities to the Hittite treaties. After the demands of the covenant were set out in speech, the people responded and accepted its terms. Then the representatives of Israel (Moses, Aaron, Nadab, Abihu and the seventy elders), went up to eat and drink on the mount of God (Exod. 24:9-11). This was a recognised way whereby people pledged themselves by an oath when agreeing to the terms of a covenant.

At the centre of the requirements that God demanded of his people were the Ten Words (Exod. 34:28; Deut. 4:13; 10:4). Nowhere does the Bible tell us how the division into ten is to be made, and this explains why, for example, the Roman Catholic Church has a different division from Protestant churches. They were written by God on two stone tablets, that are called in Deuteronomy 'the tablets of the covenant' (Deut. 9:9, 11, 15). The box or ark in which they were placed is called 'the ark of the covenant'. The Ten Words (translated very literally from Greek into English as 'the Decalogue') contain the provisions for redeemed life under God's lordship. The actions of the people (their ethics) were determined by their religious commitment. Because they were God's covenantal people, they were called to live in a distinctive way. All the Decalogue was devoted to duty towards God, even when actions and relationships with family and others were involved.

Very soon the people rebelled against God's covenant. While Moses was still up on the mount with God, under Aaron's leadership they made a golden bull. The people bowed down to it saying: 'These are your gods, O Israel, who brought you up out of Egypt' (Exod. 32:4, 8). At first God was going to destroy the people, but when Moses made intercession for the people on the basis of God's covenant with Abraham, Isaac and Jacob, he relented. On coming down from the mount, Moses broke the two stone tablets to show that the people had rebelled and broken his covenant. New tablets were made, and God confirmed his covenant in a ceremony very similar to the one that had just taken place (Exod. 34; Deut. 9:7-21).

Life in God's covenant

In addition to the Decalogue, many other laws were given by God. These related to various aspects of social behaviour, and they were intended to show how the nation under God as its king would organise its life. They are set out in the books of Exodus, Leviticus, Numbers, and Deuteronomy. As well as applying the basic principles of the Decalogue, these laws showed that Israel had to live in a distinctive manner. In matters of food and dress, for example, Israel was not to resemble the Canaanites, nor were they to try and find a message from the Lord by using heathen magic (Deut. 18:9-13). God had spoken and his statutes stood firm. They were to be a lamp to the feet and a light to the path (Psa. 119:105).

Provision was especially made for worship, and these requirements were to last until the death of Jesus as the Messiah. Instructions were given concerning the building of the tent of meeting, with all its equipment and furniture. The very name, 'tent of meeting', was an indication of God's gracious condescension. He came, and symbolically lived in a tent like his people, foreshadowing the coming of Jesus, who took on human flesh and dwelt (literally, 'tented') among men (John 1:14). Each year had its special times when the people were to come together for the great festivals such as the Passover and the Feast of Tabernacles. Several important principles were brought out by these provisions. By means of the instruction given by priests and prophets Israel had to understand:

- that communal worship was to be at the place God appointed, notably at the tent of meeting. In a special way it symbolised God's presence with his people and his desire to draw near to them in his grace.

- that sacrifice was an essential part of worship. They were taught that without the shedding of blood there could be no forgiveness of sins.

- that more was required than just a formal offering of sacrifice. There had to be a humble and contrite heart in coming to seek God's favour.

- that the blood of bulls and goats could never take away sin. All the sacrifices were imperfect, and through using the sacrificial system, the people were taught to look for a day when God would finally remove sin. The

New Testament shows us how this was fulfilled when Jesus offered himself as the great and final sacrifice for sin (Heb. 10:1-14).

For further reading

- Stuart Bonnington and Joan Milne, editors, *Love Rules: The Ten Commandments for the 21st Century* (Edinburgh: The Banner of Truth Trust, 2006).

- Graeme Goldsworthy, *According to God's Plan: The Unfolding Revelation of God in the Bible* (Leicester: IVP, 1991), pp. 167-179.

9

Worship in Ancient Israel

FROM the time of Moses worship in Israel took on new features, and because these are so important fuller comment on them is necessary.

One very significant aspect was its corporate nature. No longer was it just a matter of families worshipping separately, but provision was made for the assembly of the covenantal people. From later references it is clear that the assembly or congregation was a standard feature of life in Israel (see Psa. 22:22, 25; 35:18; 40:9; 107:32; 149:1; Joel 2:16; Mic. 2:5). The focal point of the assembly was the tent of meeting (or 'tabernacle', as many English versions call it), and it symbolised the central features of the relationship between God and his people. He dwelt among his people, and he spoke to them there. This fact is demonstrated very clearly in the provision of the temporary tent outside the camp of Israel when the covenant was broken at Sinai (Exod. 33:7-11). Once the covenant was renewed, the real tent—the instructions concerning which had already been given in Exodus 25–31—could now be built (Exod. 35–40).

The tent of meeting

Various names are used for the tent of meeting, the special place where God met with his people. It is called 'the tent of meeting', 'the dwelling place', 'the holy place', and 'the tent of testimony'. These names indicated different aspects of the function of the tent. The first one indicates God's desire to come and draw near to his people. The word 'meeting' comes from a verb in Hebrew that has the idea of making an appointment. Israel met with God at the tent by divine appointment. The word 'dwelling place' comes from a verb that means 'to dwell', so that it stresses the idea of God's abiding presence with his people. The term 'holy place' draws attention to God's holiness, while 'tent of testimony' showed that God's word had to be the guide for the lives of his people. Within the Most Holy Place was the ark of the covenant that contained the tablets of the covenant, while the book of the law (probably the whole of Deuteronomy) was placed beside it (Deut. 31:26).

In the time of Solomon the tent (that could be dismantled and then moved) gave way to the more permanent structure of the temple. This temple, destroyed by the Babylonians in 586 BC, was rebuilt after the exile, and it stood until destroyed by the Romans in 70 AD. When speaking with the Jews, Jesus indicated that the temple was giving way to the final and complete expression of God's presence in his own person (John 2:18-25), even though his own disciples could not understand this until after his resurrection. By taking on human flesh Jesus came to dwell with his people (John 1:14), and by his Spirit he still abides with them. Therefore the apostle John says: 'The dwelling place (Greek, 'tent') of God is with men' (Rev. 21:3).

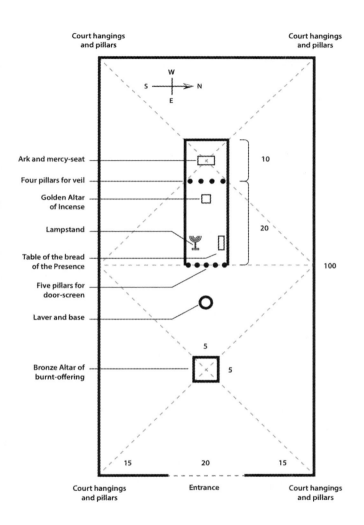

Court hangings and pillars

Court hangings and pillars

W

S — N

E

Ark and mercy-seat

10

Four pillars for veil

Golden Altar of Incense

20

Lampstand

Table of the bread of the Presence

100

Five pillars for door-screen

Laver and base

5

Bronze Altar of burnt-offering

5

15

20

15

Court hangings and pillars

Entrance

Court hangings and pillars

Diagram of the Tent of Meeting

Measurements are in cubits. One cubit = 17.5 in / 44.4 cm.

Priests

While Moses at first served as a priest, he ceased to do so when he established the office of priesthood (Exod. 29:1), and ordained his brother Aaron as priest (Lev. 8:2-36). Moses had served as a priest on Mount Sinai (Exod. 24:3-8), supervising the work of the young men as they prepared the sacrifices. Later, he also showed that the priest's work involved intercession, as he pled with God on behalf of the disobedient people (Exod. 32:11-13; Deut. 9:18, 19).

While the main function of the priest was to serve as a mediator between God and the people, it is clear that they had other roles as well. In some ways they acted like the prophets, just as Moses did after the incident of the golden calf in calling the people to repentance and submission. Part of their ministry was teaching the decrees the Lord had given (Lev. 10:11). They may well, in addition to all the work involving sacrifices, have played an important role as resident and itinerant instructors in the law (see 2 Chron. 17:8, 9; 19:8; Ezra 7:6; Jer. 18:18; Mal. 2:7).

No human priest is now required because Jesus made the perfect and final sacrifice of his own blood (Heb. 7:27; 9:28). He was both priest and sacrifice. All that the Old Testament priests did was ultimately fulfilled in Jesus our High Priest. He is very different from the priests in Israel because he is 'holy, blameless, pure, set apart from sinners, exalted above the heavens' (Heb. 7:26). In heaven, he continues now as our intercessor.

The ritual of sacrifice

Many details about the sacrifices were specified for Israel by God. They were required because no one could come before God with their hands empty (Exod. 23:15; Deut. 16:16). Some of the sacrifices were blood offerings, dealing with the forgiveness of sins, while others called peace or fellowship offerings were eaten in a communal meal to show that fellowship with God had been restored. There were daily, weekly, and annual offerings. Whatever was offered had to be the best. There should be no blemished offerings (Lev. 1:3; 3:1; Deut. 15:21, and repeated in many other places), though clearly at times the people infringed this rule (Mal. 1:6-14).

The highlight of the whole system of sacrifices was the Day of Atonement (Lev. 16), *Yom Kippur*, as modern Jews still call it following the Hebrew expression. On that day the high priest presented offerings for himself and for his family, before sacrificing two goats. One goat was slaughtered as a sin offering for the people and its blood taken into the Most Holy Place, and sprinkled on the cover of the ark. The other goat was taken away into the wilderness by the hand of some good man, symbolically carrying away the sins of the people. While the first goat showed how forgiveness was obtained (by the shedding of blood), the second goat demonstrated the reality of forgiveness (sin was carried away as far as the east is from the west, Psa. 103:12).

Symbols and types

The sacrifices of the Old Testament time were not *real* sacrifices. Just as the Lord's Supper does not have the real body and the real blood of Jesus, so the sacrifices were only *symbols* of great truths, and because they were symbols they could also serve to point forward as *types* to Jesus and his sacrifice.

A symbol is a thing or action that portrays in picture language some religious truth. That truth is a present reality at the time the symbol is employed. Thus, for the Old Testament, the slaying of an animal in sacrifice symbolised the truth that God would accept a substitute in place of a sinner. The symbols were of various kinds. There were those like the rainbow (Gen. 9: 12-16), or the stairway at Bethel (Gen. 28:10-22, and compare John 1:50). Many of the symbols were connected with the sacrifices, or with the institutions of prophet, priest, and king. Various events such as the exodus also served to symbolise aspects of God's redemption.

Many of the symbols, though not all of them, pointed forward to an aspect of *the same truth* being pictured that would only come to pass in the time of the Messiah. While speaking of these truths to the people who used the symbols, they also served to point ahead as types of Jesus. They can, therefore, be described as acted-out prophecies concerning redemption. They were pictures of what God would do through the coming of Jesus. The diagram opposite sets out this relationship using the Day of Atonement as an example, and shows how objects and actions in the Old Testament could be both symbols and types.

How could people in the Old Testament realise that something was pointing to Jesus? The very fact that the sacrifices were so imperfect and needed repetition must have awakened in many the realisation that they were pointing to something fuller and better. Also, we must think of the role of prophets

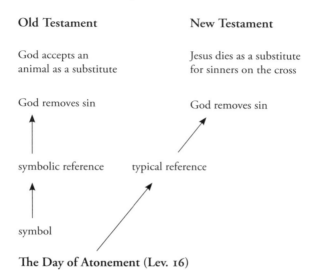

Old Testament	New Testament
God accepts an animal as a substitute	Jesus dies as a substitute for sinners on the cross
God removes sin	God removes sin
symbolic reference	typical reference
symbol	

The Day of Atonement (Lev. 16)

and priests as teachers. Just as we have preaching to instruct us about the significance of Jesus' death as symbolised in the Lord's Supper, so at that time the people had teachers to help them understand the meaning of the sacrificial system. The prophets taught that God's servant, the Messiah, would be put to death in order to take away our iniquities (Isa. 53), and that in one dramatic day a fountain would be opened for sin and uncleanness (Zech. 13:1).

For further reading

- E. P. Clowney, *Preaching and Biblical Theology* (London: Tyndale Press, 1979).

LEARNING ABOUT THE OLD TESTAMENT

- E. P. Clowney, 'Preaching Christ from All the Scriptures', Samuel T. Logan, ed., *The Preacher and Preaching: Reviving the Art in the Twentieth Century* (Phillipsburg: P&R Publishing Company, 1986), pp. 163-191.

- Samuel Schultz, *Leviticus: God Among His People, Everyman's Bible Commentary* (Chicago: Moody Press, 1983).

The Conquest and the Period of the Judges

The wilderness wanderings

Just over a year after the exodus from Egypt, the children of Israel left Sinai and moved north until they were on the southern edge of the land of Canaan. The fullest account of their movements in the period between leaving Sinai and finally entering Canaan is given in Numbers 10:11–36:13, with a summary statement in Deuteronomy 1:1–3:11. From Kadesh Barnea spies were sent out to investigate the land promised to them. The twelve spies all reported that the land was exceedingly fruitful, but that it was occupied by groups of strong and powerful people. Caleb encouraged the people to go in and take possession of the land (Num. 13:30-33), and in this he was joined by Joshua (Num. 14:6-8). The people as a whole rebelled against the Lord, at first refusing to enter Canaan, and then sinfully going in without Moses, or the presence of the ark of the covenant (Num. 14:41-45). They were defeated, and then they had to spend thirty-eight years wandering in the wilderness before they entered Canaan from the east.

After those years in the desert, the Israelites moved first to the east and then to the north of the Dead Sea, crossing the territories of Edom and Moab, before defeating the Amorite kings, Sihon of Heshbon and Og of Bashan. The captured territories were allotted to the tribes of Reuben and Gad, with half the tribe of Manasseh also receiving its territory. When the Israelites came to the plains of Moab on the east bank of the Jordan, Moses had to hand over the leadership to Joshua. God had told him earlier that because he did not honour the Lord in the incident concerning water from the rock, he was not to lead the people into the promised land (Num. 20:12). Instead, Joshua was to assume the leadership, and he would bring them into possession of the land promised long before to Abraham.

The covenant renewed

Before entering Canaan, the covenant with the Lord was renewed. Such a covenant renewal was common in the secular world of the day. Slight alterations of the requirements were also made at such a ceremony. The book of Deuteronomy as a whole forms a document detailing the covenantal renewal in the plains of Moab. After reminding the people of their recent history (chaps. 1-4), Moses again set out the Ten Words. There were slight changes to them to take account of the new situation (see Deut. 5:12-15, 21 as compared with Exod. 20:8-11, 17). Following this proclamation of God's demands, Moses expounded the significance of the Ten Words (Deut. 6–26), before making formal provision for Joshua to take over from him, and for the covenantal requirements to be taught to succeeding generations. At the end of the book of Deuteronomy, where we read of Moses' death and burial (Deut. 34), Israel had not yet come into possession of the promised land. The five books of Moses (often called the Pentateuch) end with the promises to Abraham only partially fulfilled.

The conquest

The basic theme of the book of Joshua is the fulfilment of God's covenantal promises concerning the land. This is emphasised by the accounts at the end of the book concerning the burial of Joshua, Eleazar, and Joseph (Josh. 24:29-33). These men were all buried in the land that belonged to Israel, in contrast to Abraham who had to bargain for a burying place for his wife (Gen. 23:1-20).

The account of the conquest in the book of Joshua has two aspects to it. On the one hand, the stress is on the fulfilment of God's promises concerning the land (see 11:23; 14:13-15; 21:43-45). The Israelites achieved possession of the land from the desert in the south to Lebanon in the north, from the Great Sea (the Mediterranean) to the river Euphrates in the north-east (Josh. 1:4). On the other hand, the unfinished nature of the conquest is also made plain, for strong pockets of Canaanites still remained (Josh. 13:13; 15:63; 16:10; 17:12, 13; 23:4, 5). The opening chapter of the book of Judges endorses these same aspects.

The conquest proceeded in several stages. The first thing needed was to cross the Jordan River and to capture Jericho. Those men of the two and a half tribes, who already had their territory on the east bank of the Jordan, had to leave their families and possessions and take part in the battles ahead. God intervened in a miraculous way to permit the crossing of the Jordan, even though it was at flood level (Josh. 3:9-17). Jericho fell before the armies of the Lord, again with miraculous help. Joshua was acting on the instructions of the captain of the Lord's army when he gave his orders to the people (Josh. 5:13–6:27). The city and its inhabitants were destroyed, except for Rahab the harlot and her family, for she had hidden the spies who first came into the city (Josh. 2). When the city was destroyed, a curse was placed upon the man who undertook to rebuild it. That curse came to fulfilment, when in King Ahab's time a man called Hiel rebuilt Jericho (1 Kings 16:34). From Jericho, the central uplands were captured, before a southern campaign enabled Joshua to take all the territory down to and including the Negev (Josh. 10:29-43). Then the northern part of the country was taken right up to the region of Mount Hermon (Josh. 11).

Instructions had been given to Moses regarding how the territory in Canaan was to be allocated by lots, depending on the size of the tribes (Num. 26:52-56). As already noted, on the eastern bank of the Jordan the tribes of Reuben and Gad and half the tribe of Manasseh were given territory (Josh. 13:8-32). The Levites were not given any tribal land (for the tithe of the people of Israel was their inheritance—Num. 18:23, 24; Deut. 12:12—but the other half of Manasseh and the nine other tribes were given territory on the west bank of the Jordan River (Josh. 14–19). That Joshua had to rebuke these tribes for their slowness in taking up their allotments (Josh. 18:3) probably points to their reluctance to end their journey (with God's provision of food) for a life of hard labour, and a food supply dependent on their own resourcefulness.

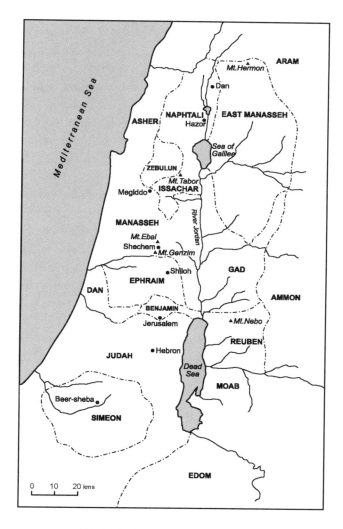

The Tribal Territorial Allocations

The Judges—preparation for kingship

The period of Israel's history in which there was rule by judges is covered in the books of Judges, Ruth and the early part of 1 Samuel. The theology of this period is summarised in Judges 2. That chapter opens with a reference to the covenantal oath regarding the land, and to the fact that Israel had already broken specific covenant provisions (verses 2, 3, compare verse 20). As part of the penalty, God was to leave the Canaanites to be a snare to them, and also as a means of testing them (verses 3, 22). In their distress, the Israelites cried to God and he saved them by raising up a deliverer or saviour. The accounts of men like Gideon and Samson are really records of how God saved his people by his chosen servants. The biblical text does not extol men like these as national heroes, but rather as instruments in God's hand to provide salvation for his people. In Judges, there is a whole series of incidents that display the same pattern. The people cry to God in their distress, he provides help, and then there is further unfaithfulness on the part of the people.

When they were settled in the land two dangers faced Israel. From within, the faith of the Canaanites threatened Israel's commitment to the Lord, while from without, Israel's security was threatened by attacks from the surrounding nations. Without an institution like the later synagogue, the means of instructing the people were limited and not well organised. Superficial similarities between Israel's faith and that of the Canaanites (such as sacrifices, sanctuaries, altars, the use of the term Baal) must have attracted many. Israel had to ward off external attacks from neighbours like the Moabites, Midianites, and especially the

Philistines. By the end of the time of the judges, there was very real danger to Israel because of confrontation with the Philistines to the north, west, and south.

Towards the end of the period covered by the book of Judges various problems were present in Israel, notably religious (Judg. 17), political (Judg. 18), and moral ones (Judg. 19). The people were clearly dissatisfied, especially with the political situation. Three times the author of Judges expresses it in this way: 'In those days Israel had no king; everyone did what was right in his own eyes' (Judg. 17:6; 18:1; 19:1). The same statement is used to end the whole book (Judg. 21:25). This meant that everyone was his own king. The book of Judges graphically illustrates what this entailed for Israel. An invitation was given to Gideon to become king (Judg. 8:22-23) but he rejected it. Their experiences of being their own kings made the people all the more ready to look for a king of God's appointment.

For further reading

- D. Ralph Davis, *Joshua: No Falling Words* (Fearn: Christian Focus, 2006).

- D. Ralph Davis, *Judges: Such a Great Salvation* (Fearn: Christian Focus, 2007).

- Rhett P. Dodson, *Every Promise of Your Word: the Gospel According to Joshua* (Edinburgh: The Banner of Truth Trust, 2016).

11

The Introduction of Kingship

Preparation for kingship

In the period of the patriarchs, God had indicated that in time to come kings would be functioning in Israel. He promised Abraham that kings would come forth from him (Gen. 17:16), while Jacob, on his return from Mesopotamia, was given a similar promise (Gen. 35:11). At the end of the Song of Moses the people sang: 'The LORD will reign for ever and ever' (Exod. 15:18). However, Moses gave explicit instructions concerning the kingship that God would eventually institute in Israel. The future introduction of kingship was clearly in God's purposes, and Moses set out the character and conduct of the king who should be appointed over Israel (Deut. 17:14-20). The prevailing practices of Near Eastern monarchs were certainly something to be avoided by Israel. The most important requirements were that the king could not be a foreigner but had to be an Israelite (as with the prophets, compare Deut. 18:15) and that he had to direct his own life by the copy of God's law he was to possess for his own use. The covenantal document was to be the king's guide so that he could direct the affairs of the nation in true dependence upon the Lord.

The introduction of kingship into Israel had to wait for several centuries after the conquest of Canaan. During the intervening period Israel was ruled by judges. The book of Judges describes what life was like without the monarchy. The problems that Israel experienced in the absence of a king are illustrated by all the accounts of incidents during this period. These experiences made the people more ready to look for a king and a hereditary royal family. The last of the judges was Samuel, whose judgeship overlaps in time with the latter period recorded in the book of Judges. He is specifically called a judge (1 Sam. 7:15-17), but he was more than that. He was also a prophet, being recognised as one from Dan in the north to Beersheba in the south (1 Sam. 3:20). In addition, he was also a priest (1 Sam. 9:12, 13; 13:8-13).

The request for a king

First Samuel 8 records the visit of the elders of Israel to Samuel. They requested him to appoint a king over them. The aged Samuel reacted bitterly to the request. He took it as a personal insult, and certainly he set out later to defend his own character (1 Sam. 12:1-5). However, the Lord made it plain to him that the people had not rejected him but rather that by their actions they had rejected the Lord himself. In part, Samuel's response was not in keeping with God's intentions for his people. There was nothing intrinsically wrong with the request of the elders. The difficulty lay in their motives, manner, and in the timing of their request, rather than in the fact of the request itself. The elders wanted a king:

- because they had reason to fear that Samuel's sons would succeed their father. Joel and Abijah were acting as judges at Beersheba in the south, while Samuel confined himself to a relatively small circuit in the area just north of Jerusalem. Those sons were not following in the ways of their father, and they were perverting the course of justice (1 Sam. 8:1-3).

- because the people sensed their own insecurity. They specifically referred to the fact that they wanted a king to go and lead them in their battles (1 Sam. 8:19, 20). Later Samuel also mentioned this reason to them (1 Sam. 12:12). This insecurity really stemmed from their own lack of faith in the Lord. When Nahash king of the Ammonites came against Israel, the people should have sought God's help and prayed for him to raise up a leader. Instead, they wanted the appointment of a king whom they thought would be able to save them.

- because they were not willing to wait for God's time, and so were prepared to break their covenantal commitments. The timing and manner of the request were incompatible with the covenantal relationship, and the consequence of their action was a breach of the covenant (1 Sam. 8:7; 10:19).

God's response was one of mercy. They were in great need, and just as God had looked upon his people in need in Egypt

(Exod. 2:25; 3:7-9), so he looked on them again and provided a deliverer (1 Sam. 9:16). Saul was the chosen king, and Samuel gathered all the people together at Mizpah, and there he declared to them the law of the king (1 Sam. 10:17-25). The purpose of this declaration was doubtless to set out the role of the king both for the benefit of the people and the king-designate.

The chosen king

The choice of Saul was God's immediate answer to the request of Israel. Physically he was outstanding among the people (1 Sam. 10:23, 24), and when he was presented to the people by Samuel, they all shouted, 'Long live the king!' When Nahash the Ammonite besieged Jabesh-gilead (east of the Jordan), Saul led out his men and routed the attackers (1 Sam. 11:1-11). Immediately after this battle Samuel called all the people to assemble at Gilgal, and there they renewed their allegiance to the kingdom of the Lord (1 Sam 11:14, 15). In effect this was a covenantal renewal ceremony, like that conducted by Moses in the plains of Moab (Deut. 29:1–31:29), or that by Joshua at Shechem (Josh. 8:30-35; 24:1-27). In many ways Saul had more in common with the preceding judges than he had with the later kings of Israel. For example, he exhibited the charisma typical of the judges (1 Sam. 10:23, 24; 11:5-15). However, in his personal life Saul lacked self-control, and at heart he was rebellious against God. In spite of military successes he was twice rejected by the Lord, seemingly at an interval of about twenty years (1 Sam. 13–15). In addition to the experience of the judges, Israel had now had further preparation for true kingship by having the wrong kind of king.

David's kingship

God's ultimate choice for the people was the man after his own heart, David (1 Sam. 13:14). Samuel was sent by God to Bethlehem to anoint one of Jesse's sons as king (1 Sam. 16:1-13). From that point onwards the narrative in the books of Samuel concentrates on David rather than Saul. There was a long period of hostility by Saul towards David, before the ultimate death of Saul on the mountains of Gilboa (to the south-west of the Sea of Galilee). David had the opportunity to kill Saul, but he refused to take the life of the one who was God's anointed (1 Sam. 24:4-6; 26:8-11). The men of Judah anointed David as king at Hebron (2 Sam. 2:2-4), to be followed by a later anointing there by the men of Israel (2 Sam. 5:1-5).

In many ways David was no better than Saul, for he was a murderer and an adulterer. However, the Old Testament tells us that in other respects he was far superior, principally because he repented of his wrongdoings. David was able to:

- stabilise the whole national life of Israel, probably with the help of the able men who had gathered round him when he was fleeing from Saul. He had been joined at the cave of Adullam by a group of 400 men, and the presence of so many discontents may well point to deep economic and social problems during the reign of Saul (1 Sam. 22:1, 2).

- remove the threat of the Philistines, and to conquer the last areas of Canaanite influence. Under David and his son Solomon the promised limits of the land were realised (1 Kings 4:21, 24).

- establish a dynasty that was going to endure, and from which in the fulness of time Jesus would come. God promised him a dynasty, and when he spoke through prophets such as Isaiah of the coming Messiah, the announcement was in terms of this covenant with David (2 Sam. 7:1-16; Isa. 9:6, 7). When Gabriel told Mary that she was going to give birth to Jesus, he said that Jesus would sit on David's throne and reign for ever and ever (Luke 1:30-33). At the very end of the New Testament, Jesus says: 'I am the Root and Offspring of David, and the bright Morning Star' (Rev. 22:16).

For further reading

- Mark Boda: *After God's Own Heart: The Gospel According to David* (Phillipsburg: P&R Publications, 2007).

- D. Ralph Davis, *1 Samuel: Looking on the Heart: Expositions of the Book of Samuel* (Fearn: Christian Focus, 2008).

- D. Ralph Davis, *2 Samuel: Out of Every Adversity* (Fearn: Christian Focus, 2006).

12

The Fate of the Monarchy

The transition to Solomon

David clearly intended that Solomon should be his successor. Seemingly, he had made an oath to this effect, though this is not recorded in 2 Samuel. However, Bathsheba reminded him of this when Adonijah decided to seize the kingship for himself (1 Kings 1:5-10, 17-21). Nathan the prophet knew of the oath, and he, Zadok the priest, and Benaiah, the army commander, combined in taking Solomon to Gihon and anointing him as king (1 Kings 1:38-40). When David died, Solomon immediately took over as king, though he acted in a ruthless and bloodthirsty manner in getting rid of his opposition. The period of David was the high-point in the history of Israel. In the covenant God made with him (2 Sam. 7), the messianic concept came to be stated in terms of Davidic kingship, which was thereafter regarded as the standard by which all other reigns were judged. However, the succeeding history showed there was tension between the vision set for Israel, and the reality of what actually transpired.

Solomon's reign

Things seemed so promising at the start of Solomon's reign. He had received excellent advice from his father (1 Kings 2:1-9), and at Gibeon he had pleased God with his request for wisdom (1 Kings 3:4-15). His main aim was to preserve and consolidate the gains made under David. There was a glory about Solomon's kingdom (compare Jesus' words in Matt. 6:29). He reorganised the administrative structure of the kingdom, that had twelve districts, each of which was to support the royal court for a month at a time. The army was also reorganised and strengthened, while a major building programme was carried out. The plans and preparations for building the temple had been made by David, but it was Solomon who brought it to reality (1 Kings 5–8). It was not meant to be for the greater glory of Solomon, but as a witness to the world that the God of Israel was the God over all (see 1 Chron. 22:5). Other building programmes by Solomon included his own palace, and the strongly fortified cities of Hazor, Megiddo, and Gezer (1 Kings 9:10-23).

Other aspects of Solomon's reign were not praiseworthy. His building programme placed stress on the country as a whole, for taxation had to pay for it. In addition, he had to conscript people to work on these projects. His own throne was most elaborate, quite unlike any other one known (1 Kings 10:20). His most serious sins, however, involved his numerous marriages, including one to the daughter of the Egyptian Pharaoh. As he grew older these wives led him into heathen worship, and he even built places of worship for Chemosh, the god of the Moabites, and for Molech, the god of the Ammonites (1 Kings

The Empire of David and Solomon (approx. 1000–925 BC)

11:7-8). Outwardly his kingdom seemed to bring to fulfilment the promises to Abraham, but yet it was marred by his own sinfulness. He was warned by God that after his death the kingdom would be divided, with just one tribe (Judah) left for the sake of David, God's servant (1 Kings 11:11-13). When Jeroboam, a northerner, who was in charge of the labour force for the families of Joseph, rebelled against Solomon, Ahijah the prophet repeated the warning that God had already given to Solomon (1 Kings 11:29-40). Because Solomon was trying to kill him, Jeroboam fled to Egypt and stayed there till Solomon's death.

The division of the kingdom

The faults of Solomon were serious in themselves, but they were aggravated by other factors as well. There was a long-standing jealousy between Judah and the Joseph tribes, Ephraim and Manasseh. Joseph had been given the right of the first-born in place of Reuben, and the privileged position was emphasised in Jacob's blessing (Gen. 49:22-26). Incidents such as the one concerning Achan (Josh. 7:1), who was from Judah, allowed a separation to develop between the northern tribes and Judah in the south. When Saul died David was anointed as king over Judah at Hebron (2 Sam. 2:4), but it was seven and a half years later before he was acknowledged as king over Israel (2 Sam. 5:1-5). That the kingdom was never fully integrated under David's rule is shown by the two rebellions that took place under him (see 2 Sam. 15:1-12; 20:1-26).

On the death of Solomon, Jeroboam immediately returned from Egypt and led the northern tribes in seeking an easier time under Solomon's son, Rehoboam. Acting on the advice of his young friends, and against the advice of the elders, Rehoboam threatened even harsher treatment. Immediately the northern tribes responded: 'What share do we have in David, what part in Jesse's son? To your tents, O Israel! Look after your own house, O David!' (1 Kings 12:16; and compare the similar words used earlier by Sheba, 2 Sam. 20:1). They then went to their homes, and a short time later at a formal assembly Jeroboam was appointed as king over Israel (1 Kings 12:20). Ahijah's prophecy was fulfilled, and only the tribe of Judah remained loyal to David's family. The tribe of Simeon never had a unified territorial area (see Josh. 19:1-9). It appears to have been incorporated into Judah by the time of David (1 Chron. 4:24-43). The ten northern tribes included the two Joseph tribes (Ephraim and Manasseh) and Benjamin (Psa. 80:1, 2), but excluded Levi because no territory was allocated to it. Hence, the southern kingdom consisted of only one tribe, Judah.

Clearly, then, a combination of factors played their part in the division. Jealousy of Judah was very real, for the northern tribes knew that God had 'rejected the tents of Joseph', and that 'he did not choose the tribe of Ephraim; but he chose the tribe of Judah, Mount Zion, that he loved' (Psa. 78:67, 68). The burdens of the new monarchy created a groundswell of unrest, while Solomon's sins brought God's judgment on the kingdom. God tore Israel from the house of David (2 Kings 17:21).

The divided monarchy

From the time the division in the kingdom came in 931 BC, the northern kingdom had an independent existence until it fell to

The Davidic-Solomonic Empire and the Division of the Kingdom

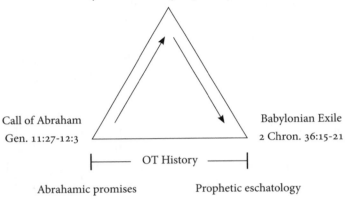

The peak in OT history
Family / land / blessing all partially fulfilled

Call of Abraham
Gen. 11:27-12:3

Babylonian Exile
2 Chron. 36:15-21

OT History

Abrahamic promises

Prophetic eschatology

the Assyrians in 722 BC. The southern kingdom of Judah lasted for another 140 years, until it fell when Jerusalem was finally destroyed by the Babylonians in 586 BC. After concentrating on David (and to a lesser extent on Solomon), the writers of the history of Israel and Judah in the books of Kings give a skeletal account of the history down to the fall of Jerusalem. Few details are given of the reigns of many kings, but attention is drawn to where further information can be found concerning them ('the annals of the kings of Israel', 'the annals of the kings of Judah'). What creates difficulty for the modern reader is that there was clearly an intention to keep a unified picture of Israel and Judah within a particular time frame. This results in the vision of the historical writer(s) switching backwards and forwards from Israel to Judah. The books of Chronicles do not give any account of the history of Israel, and even seem to deliberately avoid mention of it.

The rebelliousness of Israel

Right from the outset, Israel went its own way in religious matters. Because Jeroboam did not want his people going to Jerusalem to worship, he set up golden bulls at Bethel and Dan. In addition, he built shrines on Canaanite high places and appointed people to minister there, even though they were not from priestly families (1 Kings 12:31). The succeeding kings of Israel were like Jeroboam, and the usual comment on them is that they 'did not turn from the sins of Jeroboam' (as an example see the comment on Joram, 2 Kings 3:1-3). There was no hereditary royal family in the northern kingdom, and many of the kings died violently.

But God had not forsaken the people in Israel. Just as there were earlier prophets such as Nathan, Ahijah, and Shemaiah, major prophets such as Elijah and Elisha appear on the scene. Around 750 BC two prophets were speaking God's word to the northern kingdom (Hosea and Amos), while two others (Isaiah and Micah) were prophesying to both kingdoms. God was going to judge Israel, yet his people in Judah were not going to escape his judgment either (Amos 2:4–3:15). Promises were given that a people whom God could refer to as 'Not Loved' (*Lo-Ruhamah*) and 'Not My People' (*Lo-Ammi*) would ultimately be called 'sons

The Divided Kingdoms of Israel and Judah

of the living God' (Hos. 1:6-11, and see the quotation of this passage in Rom. 9:25, 26).

For further reading

- D. Ralph Davis, *1 Kings: The Wisdom and the Folly* (Fearn: Christian Focus, 2007).

- D. Ralph Davis, *2 Kings: The Power and the Fury* (Fearn: Christian Focus, 2007).

- Bob Fyall, *Teaching 1 Kings: From Text to Message* (Fearn: Christian Focus, 2015).

13

The Prophets

Messages from the Lord

Throughout the earlier part of Old Testament history God spoke to Israel, using individuals like Abraham or Moses as his means of communication with his people. Moses was especially favoured because the Lord spoke to him face to face, whereas other prophets did not have this closeness of fellowship (Num. 12:6-8). Because at times God used means like visions, the word used for the spokesman from God was at first 'seer' (1 Sam. 9:9). This word, and another similar one, emphasised the manner in which they received the message from God. However, the most frequent term for the spokesman came to be 'prophet'. Just as Aaron was Moses' 'prophet' (Exod. 4:16; 7:1, 2), so God used a succession of messengers called 'prophets' to speak his word to Israel and Judah.

When Israel was about to enter into the land of Canaan, in addition to making provision for kings in Israel (Deut. 17:14-20), Moses also gave God's direction concerning how the people were to receive his messages (Deut. 18:9-22). As soon as they came into the land, they would be confronted with various Canaanite practices. These practices were detestable to God, and Israel was instructed not to try and imitate them. Nine of these practices involving witchcraft and sorcery were proscribed (Deut. 18:9-13). Instead, Israel was to be blameless before the Lord, and he promised that he would give them a prophet who would declare his word. The prophet was to be:

- like Moses and to act as a spokesman for the Lord to the people.

- from among the Israelites, and not a foreigner. While a man like Balaam could be hired to speak God's message, yet he could never occupy the office of prophet (Num. 22–24).

- a person in whose mouth God would put words, and he would then speak them in God's name.

- a permanent institution in Israel to protect the Israelites, and to ensure that further teaching would be given of the basic covenantal concepts.

The passage in Deuteronomy tells of a long line of prophets that God was going to send as his messengers to Israel. However, ultimately the promise concerning the prophet was to find its fulfilment in the person of Jesus. The institution of a line of prophets was going to serve the people well, but its intention was also to point them forward to the coming of the great and final prophet. The New Testament tells us that this message in Deuteronomy found its fulfilment in the person of Jesus (Acts 3:22, 23; 7:37).

The task of the prophets

The major task of the prophet was to be a *spokesman for God*. This involved proclaiming God's word to his own generation (*forth-telling*), as well as sometimes announcing God's word concerning the future (*fore-telling*). The initial calls of both Isaiah (Isa. 6:1-7) and Jeremiah (Jer. 1:4-10) illustrate this role. In both cases their lips were touched, indicating the need for cleansing and for God's grace if they were to proclaim his message (see Isa. 6:7; Jer. 1:9). When God called a prophet he commissioned him to go and say: 'This is what the LORD says.' A clear illustration of this is contained in the words of the Lord to Amos (Amos 7:14-16). He had been a farmer, but God had called and commissioned him as his messenger to Israel.

Another task of the prophets was to *guard the kingdom of God*. They were not appointed to introduce new laws. Rather, they had to enforce the laws given through Moses long before. Thus, the last of the Old Testament prophets, Malachi, as he ended his book (Mal. 4:4), appealed to the law of Moses as the basis for the life of the people. The office of the prophet was needed to keep Israel in a true covenantal relationship with God. Often the kings tried to find political solutions to problems, while the prophets urged the people to seek the Lord and to find his will for them. Inevitably, the relationship between prophets and kings was not always good, and the prophets could never accept the separation of religion from politics. One of the terms used for the prophets ('watchmen') emphasised this task of guarding the life of the nation (see Jer. 6:17; Ezek. 3:17; 33:7). They can be viewed as covenantal enforcement mediators.

The third great task of the prophets was to *write down the history of Israel and Judah*. The books like Joshua, Judges, 1 and 2 Samuel, and 1 and 2 Kings, that we regard as historical books, are called 'the former prophets' by the Jewish people. The 'latter prophets' comprise Isaiah, Jeremiah, Ezekiel, and the twelve minòr prophets. The Jewish scholars called the historical books by this title because they regarded them as coming from the prophets, and as being written from a prophetical perspective. Thus, the historical books are interested in more than just a mere recital of facts. Often they comment on the events they are recording, and pass judgments on persons and incidents (see particularly the comments in 2 Kings 17:7-23 as to why Israel had been exiled).

The periods of prophetic activity

Although Abraham was a prophet (Gen. 20:7) and the patriarchs were in general considered to be prophets (Psa. 105:15), yet the office of prophet only came to the fore in the period marking the commencement of kingship in Israel. Hence, there was a close relationship between the institutions of prophecy and kingship. The role of the prophets differed somewhat in the later stages of Old Testament history as compared with the earlier period. From Samuel down to the series of prophets in the 8th century BC (Hosea, Micah, Amos, and Isaiah), there was stress on the spoken word of the Lord through his servants the prophets. The majority of these spoken messages are not recorded in the Bible, as God did not inspire them to be written and preserved for later generations. There are accounts of the ministries of important prophets such as Elijah and Elisha, and there are also some small prophecies by other prophets embedded in the historical books (e.g. the words of the unnamed prophet who spoke about the birth of Josiah, 1 Kings 13:1-3). The activity of various other prophets are mentioned without any extensive record of their actual words. From the middle of the 8th century BC down to the end of Old Testament history there was not only oral proclamation but written prophecies. These prophecies were addressed to the northern kingdom of Israel (and the re-united Israel after the exile), the southern kingdom of Judah, and the Gentile nations like Nineveh and Edom (compare the books of Nahum and Obadiah). They were also, during this period, the recorders of the history of Israel and Judah, and in so doing often passed judgments on the events they recounted. David is often given as the model king, and others were judged by the standard of his devotion to the Lord (see for an example 1 Kings 15:1-5 regarding Abijam).

In the earlier part of this prophetic history, the stress was more on the need for repentance towards God. However, while the later prophets do not neglect this call, yet they placed the stress on the vision of what God was going to do 'in the last days' (Heb. 1:1, 2). This expression, like other similar ones, takes on the meaning of the glorious messianic day when God would not just repair the situation of his people but do something altogether new. In that great day the sin of the people would be removed by God. Repeatedly the people were told by the prophets that God was not satisfied with sheer formality of worship, but that he desired a vital relationship with them. Such a relationship was to be expressed also in concern for the poor and the needy, and in seeing that justice was duly administered.

Commitment to God, asserted the prophets, brought with it the responsibility to live according to the demands of God's law. A redeemed people had to act justly, love mercy, and walk humbly with their God (Mic. 6:8).

For further reading

- Raymond Dillard, *Faith in the Face of Apostasy: The Gospel According to Elijah and Elisha* (Phillipsburg: P&R Publications, 1999).

- John Blanchard, *Major Themes from the Minor Prophets* (Darlington: Evangelical Press, 2012).

- John P. Milton, *Prophecy Interpreted* (London: Geoffrey Chapman, 1974).

- Douglas Stuart, 'The Prophets: Enforcing the Covenant in Israel', in Gordon D. Fee and Douglas Stuart, *How to Read the Bible for All Its Worth*, 4th ed. (Grand Rapids: Zondervan, 2014), pp. 187-211.

- E. J. Young, *My Servants the Prophets* (Grand Rapids: Eerdmans, 1952; print on demand).

14

Poets and Wise Men

Hebrew poetry

The poetry of the Old Testament is typical for the Middle Eastern region. As such, it is very different from English and other Western poetry. We depend mainly upon rhythm (a set number of syllables per line) and rhyme (the use of the same sounds at the ends of lines). These do not feature strongly in Hebrew poetry. Instead, Hebrew poetry depends upon features such as

- the extensive use of what is called parallelism. This means that after stating an idea either the opposite may be expressed (see Psa. 1:6), or perhaps the same idea is given in different words (see Psa. 24:1). The second clause in these cases may extend the idea expressed in the first clause. At other times there is the addition of complementary ideas that lead to a climax (see Psa. 29:1).

- the use of acrostics, of which Psalm 119 is the fullest. In this psalm there are twenty-two sections, following the letters of the Hebrew alphabet. In each section every verse begins with the appropriate letter of the alphabet. This distinctive feature cannot be preserved in translation into English. Other examples can be found in Psalms 9–10, Psalm 25, Psalm 34, Psalms 111–112, and Lamentations 1–3.

- the copious use of various literary features, some of which, like alliteration and assonance, are used to a much greater degree than in Western poetry.

The Psalms

One of the ways in which we respond to God's goodness and grace is by singing. While there are important songs recorded throughout the Old Testament (e.g. the Song of the Moses, Exod. 15:1-18; the song of Deborah and Barak, Judg. 5:1-31; Hannah's song, 1 Sam. 2:1-10), yet the majority are in a single collection called in Hebrew, 'Praises'. Our English word 'Psalms' comes from a Greek word meaning 'songs'. This collection of 150 songs was finalised after the return from exile in Babylon. This is demonstrated by songs such as Psalm 74, depicting the destruction of Jerusalem, or Psalm 137 ('By the waters of Babylon, there we sat down and wept'), that describes life in the exile, or Psalm 126 ('When the LORD restored the fortunes of Zion') that speaks of the joys of restoration. The earliest song in the collection is one attributed to Moses (Psa. 90). The Psalter represents, therefore, centuries of praises in Israel.

Clearly those who put the Psalter together as a collection (probably Ezra and his associates after the return from exile), did so with deliberate design. Indications of the planning behind the present structure of the Psalter include:

- the division of it into five books (Psalms 1–41; 42–72; 73–89; 90–106; 107–150), with a doxology at the end of the each section.

- the grouping together of psalms by particular composers (e.g. psalms of David, principally in Psalms 3–41, 51–71, 138–145; psalms of Asaph, Psalms 50, 73–83; psalms of the sons of Korah, Psalms 42, 44–49, 84, 87, 88).

- the deliberate linking together of psalms with similar themes (e.g. Psa. 23–24; 42–43), or those with similar titles such as the Songs of Ascent (Psa. 120–134).

There are not many indications within the Old Testament of how the Psalms were used, nor of the manner by which they were brought together to form a single collection. Reference is made in 1 Chronicles 16:8-36, Ezra 3:10-11, and Jeremiah 33:11 to the use of some parts of the Psalter. Clearly at times words were taken from several psalms and combined together as a suitable offering of praise to God (see Psa. 108, that is a combination of Psa. 57:7-11 and Psa. 60:5-12), thus forming a single new composition. Constantly they direct attention to the character of God, who stands in his majesty and holiness over against frail and sinful man. When mankind is in view, the great distinction is between the righteous and the wicked (see Psa. 1 for an excellent illustration). A living connection with the God of the covenant did not flow from human achievement but solely because of divine grace. Those who lack this living relationship with him show this by a life of systematic evil-doing. They are violent, arrogant, flattering, and plot against the righteous. They are devoid of the fear of the Lord which is the beginning of wisdom (Psa. 111:10).

The wise men and their writings

Within the Old Testament there is reference to a group of men called 'the wise', and various parts of the Old Testament, principally the books of Job, Proverbs, Ecclesiastes, and Song of Solomon, have been called 'the Wisdom books'. The wisdom spoken of in the Old Testament is presented as a gift of God, but also as wisdom that demands a response from believers. They respond with fear or reverence for God, and no term is more expressive of true love and devotion to God than this. God's wisdom is not merely theoretical but intensely practical, as it forms the foundation of all our conduct. Earlier in the Old Testament men such as Abraham and Joseph demonstrated the fear of God, just as the people of Israel as a whole did so at the time of the exodus (Exod. 14:31). The book of Deuteronomy emphasises that this fear is a result of hearing and responding to God's word (Deut. 4:10; 8:6). Solomon later prayed at the dedication of the temple in Jerusalem for all the peoples of the earth that they might know God's name and fear him (1 Kings 8:43). It is especially in some of the Psalms and in the books of Proverbs, Ecclesiastes and Job that the concept of the fear of the Lord is so central.

The wisdom books of the Old Testament differ from one another in style, but they are all directed to the same practical end.

- Job tells of an historical figure who lived in the desert east of Palestine. After the introduction (chapters 1–2) there are three cycles of speeches by Job's three friends, who argue that Job must have sinned to be suffering as he is (chapters 3–31). Then Elihu enters and takes issue with them and with Job (chapters 32–37). At last God speaks and shows Job how man's knowledge is limited. It is God who works his sovereign will, and his dealings show that he 'is full of compassion and is merciful' (James 5:11).

- Proverbs is just what the name suggests—a collection of short pithy statements. Proverbs in almost all languages are brief, are concrete not abstract, state a general truth, and often have diverse applications. The teaching of the book of Proverbs sets God's wisdom against the philosophies of the world. Fear of God was the first principle of life, and those in a right relationship with God are in a position to understand the world around them.

- Ecclesiastes presents a mirror for man, so that he can see how transient is all his work. It is only God's work that endures. The key to the book is probably the exhortation in the final chapter to seek God while one is young, so that life can be seen from a proper perspective (Eccles. 12:1-14).

- Song of Solomon is in the first instance concerned with human love and the human marriage relationship. The book constitutes powerful preaching concerning pure and true married love, that God himself has bestowed as his gift (see Song of Sol. 8:6, love 'burns like a blazing fire, like the very flame of the LORD', NIV margin). The marriage relationship is used in both Old and New Testaments to point to the loving relationship between God and his people (Hos.1–3; Jer. 2:2; 3:14; Eph. 5:22–33).

The fear of the Lord and its practical out-working in life is the dominating idea of the Wisdom books. They demonstrate what godliness in working clothes really is. Not only was it the response of faith to God, but it also provided an understanding of men and society that gave cohesion and purpose to all aspects of human life. Without the fear of the Lord, life has no satisfaction, and in the end it becomes utterly meaningless.

For further reading

- Sinclair B. Ferguson, *The Pundit's Folly: Chronicles of an Empty Life* (Edinburgh: The Banner of Truth Trust, 1995).

- Allan M. Harman, 'Approaching the Psalms', *Psalms*, vol. 1 (A Mentor Commentary: Fearn, Christian Focus Publications, 2011), pp. 17-96.

- Tremper Longman III, *How to Read Proverbs* (Downers Grove: InterVarsity Press, 2002).

- Ian McNaughton, *Opening up Job* (Leominster: Day One, 2014).

- Stephen Renn, *Song of Songs* (Bible Probe: London: Scripture Union, 1989).

15

Unveiling the Future

Prophecy

While the prophet's role was to minister God's word to his own generation, yet from its outset the institution of prophecy was concerned with prediction of the future. In Deuteronomy 18 this aspect of prophecy was expressly mentioned. Moses depicted a time in the future when the people would want to know how to distinguish between true and false prophecy. They were to be told that a false prophet's predictions would not come to pass. Such a prophet had spoken presumptuously and without divine authorisation (Deut. 18:21, 22). This type of prediction by the prophets was not necessarily to be equated with pre-written history. That is to say, when the prophets spoke of the future they did not do so in a way similar to the form of narrative used by the historical writers to record what actually happened in the history of Israel. Various factors in prophecy highlight these differences between history and prophecy, between narrative and prediction. These features are not peculiar to the Old Testament prophets, but can be seen in the prophetic ministry of Jesus (see Matt. 24–25, Mark 13), or in the book of Revelation.

- Prophecy contains many of the figures of speech that are characteristic of poetry. Thus the prophets used language that was not meant to be taken literally, but that, because of its graphic imagery, pressed home the real meaning of the message (see Isaiah's descriptions of the coming of the Assyrians in chapters 7 and 8 of his prophecy).

- In the Bible, prophecy is a wonderful combination of what is clear with what is very obscure. Enough is told in plain language of God's purposes to arouse expectation concerning the fulfilment of the prophecies. However, many of the actual details are deliberately left vague lest absolute clarity lull the people into complacency.

- In describing future events, the prophets often do not follow strict chronological order. Many of the prophets go back and take up ideas that they had already introduced in earlier passages. This means that it is impossible simply to work through a passage in the prophets and assume that the events will happen in precisely the same order as they occur in the written prophecy.

- When describing events that are far apart in time, the prophets often speak of them as if they were much closer together. Just as we have difficulty in determining any depth dimension when we look at the stars, so we find it difficult to be certain about the length of time separating specific events described in prophecy.

- The prophets looked to the Messianic age as such, and did not make any distinction between what we call the first and second comings of Christ. The New Testament clearly distinguishes between the first coming of Jesus and his coming a second time, 'not to bear sin, but to bring salvation to those who are waiting for him' (Heb. 9:28).

Apocalyptic

In addition to prophecy in the Old Testament, there are some parts that are distinctive enough from the rest of prophecy to be called apocalyptic. These passages include the book of Daniel, parts of Ezekiel and Zechariah, and a section of Isaiah that is often called 'the little apocalypse' (Isa. 24–27). Our English word 'apocalyptic' comes from a Greek word that means 'to reveal', 'to uncover'. It has been used to describe these Old Testament passages and the book of Revelation in the New Testament because it is felt that they are unveiling what is to happen in the future. This understanding of apocalyptic puts the stress on teaching about the end time as being the main characteristic of this type of literature. In so doing, there is the suggestion that prophecy and apocalyptic are not really connected with one another. This can be diagrammed in this way:

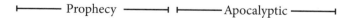

However, it is truer to say that the apocalyptic literature of the Bible is more concerned with present time rather than with future time. Its aim is to speak to the present and to explain the human situation in terms of what is to happen when God reveals the fullness of his glory and purposes to his saints in heaven. Often there is disclosure of heavenly realities by means of visions that portray the truth of God in a very vivid way. Instead of seeing a sharp distinction between prophecy and apocalyptic, we have to see them as overlapping, and this relationship can be set out in this way:

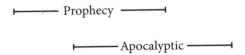

Old Testament apocalypses

In the Old Testament, the book of Daniel stands out as the major example of apocalyptic literature. During the closing years of the kingdom of Judah, Daniel was among a group of captives carried away to Babylon in 605 BC. He was soon placed in a high administrative position, and successfully served under Nebuchadnezzar, Belshazzar, and Darius. The book called by his name consists of two parts. In the first part (chapters 1-6), there is a record of various details of his life in Babylon, while the second part (chapters 7-12) contains four visions he received. In these visions there appears a succession of kingdoms arising on the earth, but also an ultimate kingdom that will last forever.

The period of Daniel was one in which God's people needed comfort and encouragement. Though warned as early as the time of Moses that disobedience would bring banishment from the promised land (see Deut. 28:64; 29:28), the people had not really believed the warnings. Even when the prophets repeated them, they 'mocked God's messengers, despised his words and scoffed at his prophets until the wrath of the LORD was aroused against his people and there was no remedy' (2 Chron. 36:16). The covenantal people were expelled from their own land and they were in captivity in Babylon. Many people must have thought that the gods of the army that could raze the temple in Jerusalem to the ground were vastly superior to the God of the Jews. Just as in the days of Moses when God displayed his power over the Egyptians and their gods, so in the time of Daniel he displayed his might by a series of miracles. These miracles, set out in Daniel chapters 1–6, show that the living God of Israel was in charge of all human affairs, and that he could deliver his people from their bondage.

By means of the visions in the second part of the book, God revealed yet again his sovereign grace, and he gave glimpses concerning the future salvation. Daniel was enabled to look forward to the coming of the Messiah, and to encourage the people with the prospect of the ultimate deliverance of God. The book ends with the mention of a mysterious time of waiting 'till the end' (Dan. 12:13). The New Testament apocalypse, the book of Revelation, takes up the message where Daniel leaves off, and points to the final confrontation between God and the forces of evil. The future is secure because 'the kingdom of this world has become the kingdom of our Lord and of his Christ, and he shall reign for ever and ever' (Rev. 11:15).

For further reading

- Joel B. Green, *How to Read Prophecy* (Leicester: IVP, 1986).

- Allan M. Harman, 'Introductory Matters', in *Daniel, Study Commentary Series* (Darlington: Evangelical Press, 2007), pp. 13-31.

- John P. Milton, *Prophecy Interpreted* (London: Geoffrey Chapman, 1954).

- Leon Morris, *Apocalyptic* (Grand Rapids: Eerdmans, 1983).

16

The New Covenant

Covenantal history

From the time of the covenant made on Mount Sinai, Israel as God's people was expected to live in obedience to the covenant's demands. With the introduction of kingship another facet of the relationship with the Lord was stressed in the covenant with David (2 Sam. 7; Psa. 89; Psa. 132). The Davidic family was chosen to provide the line of kings that would ultimately culminate in the coming of Jesus. Throughout the Old Testament period the people often wandered far from the demands of the covenant, and one of the major tasks of the prophets was to call them back to obedience to it. A prophet like Elijah, in his dejection after reaching Horeb, could complain to God: 'I have been very zealous for the Lord God Almighty. The Israelites have rejected your covenant, broken down your altars, and put your prophets to death with the sword' (1 Kings 19:10).

Some periods of reformation took place, particularly those in the days of Hezekiah and Josiah. The reformation under Josiah is important in itself, but also because it provides a background for the teaching of Jeremiah and Ezekiel of a new covenant. Josiah reigned for 31 years (from 639 BC to 608 BC), the first eight of which were probably by means of a regent until he came of age. The biblical accounts of his reign are found in 2 Kings 22; 23:1-30; and 2 Chronicles 34–35. He adopted an independent policy for Judah that had as its aim

- freedom of control from Assyria that had already been responsible for the downfall of the northern kingdom of Israel in 722 BC

- the removal of Assyrian influence in the worship of God (the biblical records concentrate on this aspect of his reign)

- the attempt to integrate the northern part of the country that previously belonged to Israel into the kingdom of Judah.

Josiah began a work of reformation (2 Chron. 34:3-7), which was given new impetus and direction when 'the book of the law' (probably some or all of the book of Deuteronomy) was found during repairs to the temple. Even in the midst of this work, a warning was given to king and people that, though Josiah himself was going to be spared seeing the final disaster on the nation, yet God's punishment was coming on the people because of their sins (2 Kings 22:15-20). The people of Judah joined in a solemn act of covenantal renewal (2 Kings 23:1-3), and they celebrated the Passover in a manner that had not been seen since the days of the judges (2 Kings 23:21-23). But the heart of the people had not really changed at all, and so the prophets started to proclaim the message of a new covenant that God was going to introduce.

The new covenant

Earlier prophets had spoken of a new relationship with God that God himself would bring about. Prophets such as Hosea and Isaiah depicted a day coming when the worship of idols would cease, and God and his people would be bound together for ever. Thus, Hosea speaks of a future covenant that God will make, and of the time when 'I will say to Not My People, "You are my people"; and he shall say, "You are my God"' (Hos. 2:23; compare Paul's use of this passage in Rom. 9:25). Isaiah prophesied that the Messiah himself would be the covenant for the people (Isa. 42:6), and that he would confirm the sure promises made to David by means of an everlasting covenant (Isa. 55:3; see also Isa. 61:8; Jer. 32:40; 50:5; Ezek. 16:60; 37:26). The idea of 'newness' is brought out by Ezekiel's references to a 'new heart' or a 'new spirit' to be given to the people by God (Ezek. 11:19; 18:31; 36:26), just as the psalms that speak of the coming judge call for a 'new song' (Psa. 96; 98).

It is, however, in Jeremiah 31:31-34, that we have the fullest statement of the new covenant. Jeremiah was a prophet during the reign of King Josiah. He was called to the office of prophet in the thirteenth year of King Josiah (626 BC), and prophesied until the fall of Jerusalem in 586 BC. The great theme of his prophecy was the judgment of God directed against Judah, especially in the form of the invading Babylonian army. He tried to call the people back to obedience to the existing covenant, saying: 'Listen to the terms of the covenant and follow them' (Jer. 11:6).

He realised that the reforms under Josiah, while good in themselves, had not changed the basic condition of the people. In a prophecy specifically dated as being in the days of King Josiah, Jeremiah speaks the Lord's condemnation of Judah because the lessons manifest in the fall of the northern kingdom of Israel had not been taken to heart (Jer. 3:6-10). The situation required something more than just re-affirmation of the existing covenant. What was needed was a covenant that was new in character as well as new in time. Jeremiah gives a picture of days coming when God will institute a new covenant. The Lord declared: 'I will put my law in their minds, and write it on their hearts. I will be their God, and they will be my people' (Jer. 31:33). This assurance of God's special relationship with them, expressed in the oft-repeated covenant formula of the Old Testament, pointed to continuity with the past, just as there were other elements that directed attention to what was new. Several things were intended by this new covenant.

- The new covenant would mean that God would implant his law in the hearts of his people. What was needed was not just better memories, but a new nature! Only God could give a heart liberated from bondage to sin and able to respond spontaneously to his commands.

- The new covenant would be a matter of personal experience of the living God. The relationship with God was not just to be on national terms, but it was to be a very personal matter. Every member of the covenantal community would possess knowledge of the Lord because of their new heart.

- The new covenant was to involve God granting his forgiveness and not remembering their sins any more. Clearly forgiveness was taught elsewhere and earlier in the Old Testament. But this prophecy looked forward to the day when God would act through the death of the Messiah to do something to blot out his people's sins for ever. Under the Old Testament sacrifices there was remembrance of sins every year (Heb. 10:3). Under the new covenant there is no such remembrance because of a sacrifice that was made once for all (Heb. 7:27).

The prophecy of Jeremiah 31 came to fulfilment in the ministry and death of Jesus. It is the passage that suggested to Origen (about 184–254 AD) in the early church that the last twenty-seven books of the Bible should be called 'the New Testament'. This prophecy is the largest passage of the Old Testament to be quoted in the New Testament (Heb. 8:8-12, and partially repeated in Heb. 10:16-17). It also occurs in passages dealing with the Lord's Supper (Matt. 26:28; Mark 14:24; Luke 22:20; 1 Cor. 11:25). Jesus' death inaugurated the new covenant, one that transcends the old boundaries of Israel and Judah and embraces believers of all nations.

For further reading

- W. J. Dumbrell, 'The New Covenant', *Covenant and Creation: An Old Testament Covenant Theology* (Milton Keynes: Paternoster, 2013), pp. 242-290.

LEARNING ABOUT THE OLD TESTAMENT

- F. D. Kidner, *The Message of Jeremiah* (Leicester: IVP, 1987).

17

Exile and Return

Exile from the promised land

The threat of exile was given to the children of Israel by Moses even before they entered into the land. In addition to the threat of invading armies besieging them, Moses explained that if the Lord's commands were not heeded, the people would be scattered among the nations (Lev. 26:27-33; Deut. 28:64-67). That warning was taken up and set before the people by several of the Old Testament prophets (e.g. Amos, Micah, Hosea, Isaiah). Thus, Isaiah spoke of the desolation of the land that was coming, when God would send everyone far away (Isa. 6:11-13). He also described the results of the impending Assyrian invasion (Isa. 7:18-25; 8:1-10).

The fall of Israel (the northern kingdom)

The northern kingdom of Israel was the first of the two parts of the nation to fall. The Assyrians gradually encroached on Israelite territory as Israel's power declined. Hoshea, the last king, revolted against Assyria, by refusing to pay the annual tribute money (2 Kings 17:3-4). The Assyrians marched on Israel in 724 BC, and though the Assyrians expected the city of Samaria to yield quickly to a siege, it managed to hold out until it finally fell in 722 BC. An Assyrian governor was placed over the land, many Israelites were deported, and foreign settlers were brought in (2 Kings 17:24). Israel had existed as a separate nation for over two centuries (from 931 BC to 722 BC), but now ceased for ever to be a sovereign power.

The fall of Judah (the southern kingdom)

The southern kingdom of Judah was to last for another 130 years. In 605 BC, just prior to Judah's downfall, the Babylonians under Nebuchadnezzar had become the major power. Jerusalem was captured in 596 BC, and about 10,000 people from Judah were taken away captive (2 Kings 24:14-16). Zedekiah was installed and ruled for a time, before he revolted against his overlord. Jeremiah had constantly spoken of the final doom that was ahead, and, in accordance with his word, Jerusalem fell finally in 586 BC. In addition to the very full accounts in the biblical text (2 Kings 25; 2 Chron. 36:15-21; Jer. 52), letters from the military outpost at Lachish (south-west of Jerusalem) give graphic details of the Babylonian invasion. Jerusalem was devastated, and all but the poor of the land were seized and deported (2 Kings 25:11-12, 22). That the group of deportees had to be quite large is shown by the numbers who returned from captivity in 538 BC, though admittedly the numbers could have increased considerably during the exile.

The kingdoms of Israel and Judah did not fall simply because they were too weak to withstand the major powers like

Assyria and Babylon. The biblical writers declare that it was because of the sins of the people that God permitted this to happen. Israel had practised idolatry, worshipped the stars, and sacrificed sons and daughters in the fire (2 Kings 17:7-17), all of which was a rejection of God's covenantal demands (verse 15). The invasion of Judah by the Babylonians is said to have been God's purpose to destroy Judah 'in accordance with the word of the Lord proclaimed by his servants the prophets' (2 Kings 24:2). The land had the opportunity to enjoy its Sabbath rest for seventy years in order to fulfil Moses' warning (Lev. 26:34, 43; repeated by Jeremiah, Jer. 29:10). It could then have what the people had failed in their sin to give it during their years of occupation. The reason why the smaller and weaker southern kingdom of Judah lasted longer than Israel cannot be explained in human terms. It was solely because the family of David was the divinely appointed royal household of Judah, and because of God's choice of Jerusalem that Judah lasted longer.

Conditions in exile

The cream of the Jewish population was deported to Babylon, but yet the captivity they experienced was not oppressive in many respects. They had freedom of movement, and they were able to engage in trade, commerce, and crafts. Perhaps the influence of Daniel at the Babylonian court may account for the generally favourable conditions under which the Israelites lived. They dwelt by the river (or canal) Kebar (Ezek. 1:1), that was the source of irrigation for the rich farming area. Contact was maintained with Palestine by correspondence (see Jer. 29), and messengers were also able to bring information such as the fall of Jerusalem (see Ezek. 33:21 22). As the opening of Jeremiah's letter shows, their own office-bearers such as prophets, elders, and priests were still active even in captivity.

The reality of the exile experience was, however, pressed home to the people, and they knew that it was a punishment by God. Certainly in the early years they felt deeply the experience of being severed from Jerusalem and all its religious associations. Psalm 137 records how they wept when, by the rivers of Babylon, they thought about Zion. The book of Lamentations also records the outpourings of a devout heart in the face of the destruction of Jerusalem. The poet speaks of how God had deserted his sanctuary and allowed evil forces to destroy it. The sin of the people had brought this destruction to pass. The small prophecy of Obadiah most probably comes from this period. Obadiah refers to the sin of the Edomites in rejoicing at their brother's fall, which point is referred to in Psalm 137:7 ('Remember, O Lord, what the Edomites did on the day Jerusalem fell. "Tear it down", they cried, "tear it down to its foundations!"'). Even after Jerusalem had fallen, the exiles found it difficult to understand the need for spiritual change and obedience to the Lord (Ezek. 33:30-33).

The return from captivity

Repeatedly the prophets had spoken of the fact that God was going to bring Israel and Judah back from their captivity. Isaiah in particular had described not only a return to Palestine but also a return to the mighty God (Isa. 10:21). In his later pictures of the return, he describes the new exodus that was going to take place, when God would bring his people through the desert to the promised land. Both Jeremiah and Ezekiel prophesied concerning the return, with Ezekiel stressing the return of *one nation*, under *one king* (Ezek. 37:1-28). Not only were there general prophecies depicting the return, but Isaiah went further and spoke of how God would accomplish it. He said that God would raise up an anointed servant called Cyrus who would permit the return and the rebuilding of the temple (Isa. 44:28–45:7).

Cyrus the Persian captured Babylon in 539 BC, and in 538 BC he issued a decree permitting the return of the Jews (see 2 Chron. 36:22, 23; Ezra 1:1-4). This marked the end of the period of exile. The actual return took place in three phases, and these were characterised by:

- the return in 537 BC under Sheshbazzar, and, after opposition, the completion of the rebuilding of the temple (Ezra 1–6). The prophets of this stage were Haggai and Zechariah, who encouraged the people in their work on the temple.

- the return in 458 BC under Ezra, and an account of his reforms especially in the area of mixed marriages (Ezra 7–10). The book of Esther is dated in the period just prior to this return, and it gives a picture of Jewish life under Persian rule.

- the final return under Nehemiah in 444 BC, and the rebuilding of the walls of Jerusalem (Ezra 4:6-23; Neh. 1–12). The last prophet of the Old Testament, Malachi, most probably worked in the period of Nehemiah.

The joy of the returning exiles is captured in Psalm 126. For them it was like a dream to have been restored by the Lord to their own land. They could sing: 'The LORD has done great things for us; we are glad' (verse 3).

For further reading

- Roger Ellsworth, *Opening Up Malachi* (Leominster; Day One Publications, 2007).

- Roger Ellsworth, *Opening up Zechariah* (Leominster; Day One Publications, 2010).

- John Sailhamer, *First and Second Chronicles* (Chicago: Moody Press, 1983).

- Peter Williams, *Opening up Haggai* (Leominster; Day One Publications, 2008).

18

The Promised Messiah

Expecting the Messiah

Some believers in the period just before Jesus' birth had a strong sense of expectancy regarding the coming of the Messiah. The aged Simeon had been told that he would not die before he saw the Lord's Christ (Luke 2:26). Similarly, Anna spoke of the birth of Jesus to all who were looking for God's redemption (Luke 2:38). But the expectation was far wider than with a small group of devout worshippers. Many Jewish people were looking for the appearance of the Messiah, though they disputed whether Jesus was indeed that person. John 7:25-31 records incidents concerning Jesus' public ministry. Some of the people responded to his teaching by claiming he was the Christ. Others said: 'How can Christ come from Galilee? Does not the Scripture say that the Christ will come from David's family and from Bethlehem, the town where David lived?' (verses 41, 42)

During his ministry Jesus taught that people should have known about his coming because they had the writings of the Old Testament. Because by his teaching he clearly made himself equal with God, the Jews were roused to anger. In replying to them Jesus said: 'You diligently study the Scriptures because you think that by them you possess eternal life. These are the Scriptures that testify about me, yet you refuse to come to me to have life' (John 5:39, 40). Jesus repeatedly spoke of the fact that the Old Testament Scriptures expressly taught about his coming and his mission. After his resurrection, in speaking with Cleopas and his friend on the road to Emmaus, Jesus began with Moses and all the prophets and explained what was said in all the Scriptures about himself (Luke 24:27). A little later, to the assembled disciples, he said: 'Everything written about me in the Law of Moses and the Prophets and the Psalms must be fulfilled' (Luke 24:44).

Pointers to the Messiah

Throughout the Old Testament there were signposts directing people to the coming of a deliverer. From the earliest promise in Genesis 3:15 onwards, God indicated in various ways that he was going to save his people. As the centuries passed it was more clearly revealed that this was to be done through an individual figure, anointed for the particular mission on which he would be sent. The Hebrew word for 'anointed' has been taken over into English as 'Messiah', while our word 'Christ' is simply the Greek equivalent. In Jacob's blessing of his sons, he indicated that the sceptre was not going to depart from the tribe of Judah until the one came to whom tribute belonged (Gen. 49:10). Similarly, in another cryptic statement, Balaam spoke of his vision of a star coming out of Jacob (Num. 24:17).

Alongside such earlier prophecies we have to consider the role played by the sacrificial system in Israel. In the sacrifices Israel had picture language, that both taught them about the reality of sins forgiven, and also pointed them ahead to a far greater sacrifice for sins. The constant repetition of sacrifices demonstrated the inability of these sacrifices to take away sins. What was needed was for God in his grace to provide a single sacrifice for sin that would not need any repetition. The prophets spoke of a glorious day in the future when God himself would open up a fountain to cleanse the people from their impurity and sin (Zech. 13:1). This was fulfilled when Jesus died once for all for the sins of his people (Heb. 7:27).

The offices of prophet, priest, and king also pointed forward to someone who would both fulfil each office, and would also combine them in one person. The holders of these offices in the Old Testament period were all imperfect, but yet the offices pointed away from the occupants to the coming fulfilment. The New Testament tells how they were all fulfilled in Jesus. He came as the last of a long line of prophetic messengers (Matt. 21:33-45), and so was the culmination of the promise of a prophet like Moses (Deut. 18:18; Acts 3:22, 23). As a priest, Jesus was not only the offerer of a sacrifice, but he himself was that sacrifice. Peter points to this fact when he says that 'he himself bore our sin in his body on the tree, so that we might die to sins and live for righteousness' (1 Pet. 2:24). To Jesus as king all authority has been given (Matt. 28:18), and he must reign until all his enemies are subdued under his feet (1 Cor. 15:25).

The Suffering Servant

All the early indications in the Old Testament of a coming saviour were made explicit by the great prophets of the eighth century BC. Amos and Hosea, Micah and Isaiah unite in their predictions concerning an individual messianic figure. On many occasions they use language from earlier in the Old Testament, and they show how it relates to the promised Messiah.

Hosea spoke of a period when the Israelites would lack a king, and then they would 'return to seek their God and David their king' (Hos. 3:4, 5). Amos also connects the family of David with the coming days of blessing (Amos 9:11, 12), while Micah told of a ruler over Israel who was going to come from Bethlehem of Judah (Mic. 5:2). King Herod heard of this passage when he enquired of the priests and teachers where the Christ should be born. 'In Bethlehem in Judea', they answered, and then quoted this verse from Micah (Matt. 2:1-6).

But, above all the other prophets, Isaiah proclaimed most fully the character and work of the coming Messiah. At a crucial point in Judah's history he prophesied of a virgin who would bear a son to be called Immanuel, God-with-us (Isa. 7:14). That child was going to bear names that belong only to God, for he was to be Wonderful Counsellor, Mighty God, Everlasting Father, Prince of Peace. Moreover, his task was described in kingly terms, and he was to sit on David's throne (Isa. 9:6, 7). This coming ruler from the stump of Jesse would rule righteously, and gather many nations under his banner (Isa. 11:1-16).

Isaiah describes very fully in the Servant Songs the role of this special servant whom God would anoint as his Messiah.

These songs are found in Isaiah 42:1-9; 49:1-13; 50:4-11; 52:13-53:12; and 61:1-4. The term 'servant of the LORD' is used in the Old Testament very rarely. It is applied to special servants such as Moses and David, and sometimes even to the nation as a whole. But as Isaiah's prophecies proceed, we hear him speaking of an individual who is truly Israel and who pours out his soul to death for many (Isa. 53:12). The fourth servant song gives us five pictures of the promised Messiah.

- It summarises the priestly work that the Messiah will carry out (52:13-15).

- It speaks of unbelief when he appears and of his unpromising appearance (53:1-3).

- It describes him as a substitute for sinners who have wandered away (53:4-6).

- It tells of his submissiveness and purity even in death (53:7-9).

- It predicts his successful intercession (53:10-12).

The focal point of both Old and New Testament is the same—Jesus, the Saviour. In answer to a question from the Ethiopian official about Isaiah 53, 'Philip began with that very passage of Scripture and told him the good news about Jesus' (Acts 8:35). As Augustine put it: 'The New is in the Old concealed; the Old is in the New revealed.' Study of the Old Testament must always lead us to Christ, and to that gospel that God 'promised beforehand through his prophets in the Holy Scriptures regarding his Son, who as to his human nature was a descendant of David' (Rom. 1:2, 3).

For further reading

- Peter Lillback, editor, *Seeing Christ in All the Scripture: A Concise Guide to Reading the Bible* (Glenside, PA: Westminster Seminary Press, 2016).

- Darrell L. Bock and Mitch Glaser, editors, *The Gospel According to Isaiah 53* (Peabody: Hendrickson, 2012).

- E. P. Clowney, *The Unfolding Mystery: Discovering Christ in the Old Testament* (Phillipsburg: P&R Publications, 1988).

- Allan A. MacRae, *The Gospel of Isaiah* (Chicago: Moody Press, 1977).

- Chris Wright, *Knowing Jesus through the Old Testament: Rediscovering the Roots of Our Faith* (London: Marshall Pickering, 1992).

19

Preaching from the Old Testament

THE Scriptures of the Old Testament are not given to satisfy our curiosity about Jewish history. They are a record of God's covenantal dealings with his people before the coming of Christ. The contents of the Old Testament are 'to teach us, so that through endurance and the encouragement of the Scriptures we might have hope' (Rom. 15:4). We have to read and learn from them, just as those in the early church did. In particular, they have to be part of the teaching material for Christians today, and an essential part of the content of our preaching. The Old Testament was *the* Bible for our Lord and the early church.

Differences between preaching from the Old and New Testaments

While all preaching has many similarities, yet there are noticeable differences when preaching from Old Testament passages as compared with preaching from the New Testament. The time frame of the Old Testament is much longer, as the period for which we have extra-biblical information (from Abraham to

Nehemiah) is at least 1,600 years. Many different cultural settings are covered, as the geographic scope of Old Testament moves from Mesopotamia to Palestine to Egypt. The nature of the Old Testament, the bulk being narrative, means that while units are selected for preaching, they will be much larger than those selected for preaching from the New Testament. For the latter, the unit may be a parable, or an incident in the Gospels, or a sentence in an epistle, or even a phrase containing rich doctrinal teaching. However, for the Old Testament the unit will quite often be a chapter, or in the case of smaller books, the entire book.

But the greatest difference between the two is that the Old Testament deals with God's revelation *before* the coming of Christ, not *after* his coming. We must always keep this difference in view when preparing to preach from the Old Testament, for we cannot use Old Testament passages as if they were given post-Calvary. They have to be explained in their own context, and then related to later biblical revelation concerning God's saving mercy. New Testament explanations should not be arbitrarily imposed on Old Testament passages.

Respect for Old Testament literary types

When a choice has been made of an Old Testament passage on which to preach, then we must ask ourselves, 'What type of biblical revelation is this?' The reason for this question is that our approach to the text will differ to some extent whether it is narrative, poetry (see pp. 91-92), or prophecy (see pp. 85-88). God has chosen to give us his revelation in different forms, and these have to be respected and used appropriately. For example, just because an incident is recorded in biblical narrative does not automatically mean that the actions described there are for us to imitate. Many biblical narratives do not draw out the implications of the actions, nor explain how they fit into the overall flow of God's revelation. Similarly, not every statement in a poetical passage can be taken in a literal way, for poetry uses similes ('like a mountain') and metaphors ('God is a fortress') to convey truth.

Prophecy has its own difficulties of interpretation. First of all, much prophecy was given in poetical form, so it shares all the features found in other songs in the Old Testament, including the entire book of Psalms. Moreover, prophecy was first of all directed to the prophet's own contemporaries, and revelation regarding the future is often couched in language that lacks precision as to dates and personalities.

These comments are not intended to divert you from preaching on the Old Testament, but merely to alert you to the need to be aware of the different ways in which God has given us his inspired teaching. The intrinsic nature of the various literary types has to be respected, and that will determine some of our interpretation. But other facts show us the help there is within Scripture itself when we come to preach from the Old Testament, and some of these will now be discussed.

The analogy of Scripture

This term, which has been used since the Reformation, simply means that we have to keep in mind the teaching of *all the*

Scripture. No passage of the Bible can be truly understood when extracted from its context, or isolated from the overall thrust of its teaching. The biblical books fit together as a unit, and difficult passages are to be explained by reference to those where the teaching is plain. Sometimes clarity is provided by a later passage in the same book, or by comment made by another biblical author.

God's revelation did not come all at one time. It came progressively, so that revelation has a history to it. The individual books of the Old Testament were inspired by God, and they were recognised as such by the believing community before the final group of thirty-nine books were brought together as 'the Scripture' (John 10:35; 2 Tim. 3:16), 'the very words of God' (Rom. 3:2).

What is so important also is to see how the Lord Jesus and his apostles understood and applied the Old Testament. They are the inspired interpreters of Moses and the prophets (Luke 16:29), and Christian teaching must focus on all that is written about Christ in the law of Moses, the prophets, and the psalms (Luke 24:44). The books of the Old Testament are God-breathed, and are 'profitable for teaching, for reproof, for correction, and for training in righteousness' (2 Tim. 3:16).

Help from biblical theology

Any passage chosen from the Old Testament as a preaching unit must be set in its place within the unfolding biblical theology contained in it (see the earlier discussion on pp. 4-6). As an illustration, it is inappropriate to take part of the story of Noah in Genesis and attempt to understand it as if it came from the period of Isaiah or Malachi. There was a progressive unfolding of God's purposes at each stage that amplified and extended the revelation that had already been given. This fact must be recognised, for it is basic to a true approach to the text of the Old Testament.

Moreover, at each stage of the Old Testament, as marked out by the making of covenants between God and his people (see pp. 15-19), the revelation pointed forward to something greater and more glorious to come. What God had done in the past, he was going to do on a more wonderful scale in the future. The God who redeemed Israel from Egypt was going to redeem a people for himself out of all nations.

We have already seen earlier in this book, how God prepared for the coming of the Lord Jesus by giving his people ritual acts of worship (such as sacrifice), and also by appointing priests, prophets, and kings whose offices foreshadowed those that the Lord Jesus would hold. He is the perfect priest, the last and greatest prophet, and the king whose rule will be eternal.

The Old Testament certainly points forward to the Lord Jesus, though not expressly on every page. God's covenantal promises and his saving intervention in the life of his people provided hope for the future. From a Christian perspective we can preach on Old Testament passages, drawing out their significance for contemporaries, but we can also point to their fulfilment in Christ. The focal point of both testaments is the Lord Jesus, the only redeemer.

LEARNING ABOUT THE OLD TESTAMENT

Asking the right questions

When we have chosen a passage on which to preach, and decided, after prayer and study, what it means, we must ask some questions.

- Does the interpretation do justice to the words of the passage and their intent?

- Is the interpretation in keeping with the context?

- Have we taken into account the type of literature from which it comes?

- Does the view we have adopted of the passage fit in with the biblical theology of the period?

- How does the passage relate to the coming and ministry of the Lord Jesus?

- Are we able to deal with it, not merely as Old Testament literature, but as a passage with a Christian message for today?

Many more aspects of preaching from the Old Testament need exploration. This brief introduction requires supplementation from other discussions that enlarge and develop ideas presented here. The books listed below provide much help as you try and find ways in which to teach and preach from the Old Testament in an overtly Christian way.

For further reading

- D. Ralph Davis, *The Word Became Fresh: How to Preach from Old Testament Narrative Texts* (Fearn: Christian Focus Publications, 2007).

- F. D. Kidner, *Preaching from the Old Testament* (Edinburgh: Rutherford House, 1983).

- Allan M. Harman, 'Preaching from the Psalms', in *Preaching the Word: Essays in Honour of Professor Tom Wilkinson on His 90th Birthday* (Brisbane: 2006), pp. 15-23.

- J. A. Motyer, *Preaching? Simple Teaching on Simply Preaching* (Fearn: Christian Focus, 2013).

- O. Palmer Robertson, *Preaching Made Practical* (Welwyn Garden City: EP Books, 2015).

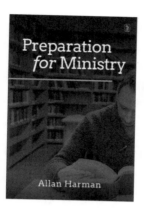

Preparation for Ministry

Allan Harman

Preparation For Ministry deals with important issues relating to a call to the Christian ministry, theological training, and entry into pastoral work.

The author has written it out of his own rich experience as a student, a pastor, and a seminary teacher. Those contemplating entry into the Christian ministry will benefit greatly from his practical advice on such subjects as coming to faith, the call to the ministry, pre-theological study, and choosing a theological college or seminary.

A brief bibliography is provided, and the book also contains useful appendices, including:

a guide to preparatory reading

a short guide to sermon preparation

C. H. Spurgeon's *The Minister's Self-Watch*

B. B. Warfield's *The Religious Life of Theological Students*

ISBN 978 1 84871 6 230 | 124 pp. | small paperback

Weeks: Gateway to the Old Testament

Gateway to the Old Testament

Noel Weeks

This book will serve as an introduction to the literature and message of the Old Testament in general, but it also provides a more detailed study of the three foundational books-Genesis, Exodus and Deuteronomy-on which the rest of the Bible stands.

Those who are new to the study of the Bible will find that *Gateway to the Old Testament* will help to build a secure and lasting foundation for a life-time of study, while others for whom the Old Testament is already a well-known companion will find insight which will help towards a deeper and even more rewarding grasp of the message of Scripture as a whole.

Includes:

> Survey of the whole Old Testament
> Detailed studies of Genesis, Exodus, and Deuteronomy
> Questions for discussion

ISBN 978 0 85151 6 905 | 320 pp. | small paperback

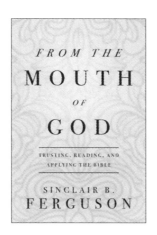

From the Mouth of God:
Trusting, Reading, and Applying the Bible

Sinclair B. Ferguson

THE BIBLE—

Why should we believe—as Jesus did—that it is 'the mouth of God'?
When did it come into existence?
Is it inerrant?
What do we need to learn in order to understand it better?
How does its teaching change our lives?

In *From the Mouth of God*, Sinclair B Ferguson answers these and other important questions about trusting, reading, and applying the Bible.

ISBN 978 1 84871 2 423 | 224 pp. | paperback

The New Testament:
An Introduction to its Literature and History

J. Gresham Machen

The writing of John Gresham Machen was characterized by clarity of thought, depth of scholarship, and an evident passion for the message of the Bible. It is a mark of his peculiar gifts that none of these features is lacking in these chapters of New Testament Introduction.

These pages are a valuable part of Machen's witness to the integrity, magnificence, and plentitude of the writings that constitute the New Testament.

ISBN 978 0 85151 4 499 | 386 pp. | paperback